THE POLEMICS
AND
POEMS OF
Rachel Speght

EDITED BY

Barbara Kiefer Lewalski

New York   Oxford
OXFORD UNIVERSITY PRESS

1996

For Kenneth and David Lewalski

Oxford University Press

Oxford   New York

Athens   Auckland   Bangkok   Bombay
Calcutta   Cape Town   Dar es Salaam   Delhi
Florence   Hong Kong   Istanbul   Karachi
Kuala Lumpur   Madras   Madrid   Melbourne
Mexico City   Nairobi   Paris   Singapore
Taipei   Tokyo   Toronto

and associated companies in

Berlin   Ibadan

Library of Congress Cataloging-in-Publication Data
Speght, Rachel
The polemics and poems of Rachel Speght / edited by Barbara Kiefer
Lewalski.
p.   cm. — (Women writers in English 1350–1850)
Includes bibliographical references and index.
ISBN 0-19-508614-7 (cloth)—ISBN 0-19-508615-5 (paper)
1. Women—Poetry. 2. Feminism—England—History—17th century—
Sources.   I. Lewalski, Barbara Kiefer, 1931– .   II. Title.
III. Series
PR2349.S74A6   1996
821'.3—dc20   95-47244

1   3   5   7   9   8   6   4   2

Printed in the United States of America
on acid-free paper

CONTENTS

Approximations of the title pages of Speght's works appear on pages 1, 29, and 43.

FOREWORD

Women Writers in English 1350–1850 presents texts of cultural a
literary interest in the English-speaking tradition, often for the fi
time since their original publication. Most of the writers represented
the series were well known and highly regarded until the profession
ization of English studies in the later nineteenth century coincid
with their excision from canonical status and from the majority of lite
ary histories.

The purpose of this series is to make available a wide range of unf
miliar texts by women, thus challenging the common assumption th
women wrote little of real value before the Victorian period. While
one can doubt the relative difficulty women experienced in writing f
an audience before that time, or indeed have encountered since, th
series shows that women nonetheless had been writing from early c
and in a variety of genres, that they maintained a clear eye to reader
and that they experimented with an interesting array of literary strat
gies for claiming their authorial voices. Despite the tendency to tre
the powerful fictions of Virginia Woolf's *A Room of One's Own* (192
as if they were fact, we now know, against her suggestion to the co
trary, that there were many "Judith Shakespeares," and that not all
them died lamentable deaths before fulfilling their literary ambitions.

This series is unique in at least two ways. It offers, for the first tim
concrete evidence of a rich and lively heritage of women writing i
English before the mid-nineteenth century, and it is based on one
the most sophisticated and forward-looking electronic resources in th
world: the Brown University Women Writers Project textbase (full te
database) of works by early women writers. The Brown Universit
Women Writers Project (WWP) was established in 1988 with a gra
from the National Endowment for the Humanities, which continues t
assist in its development.

Women Writers in English 1350–1850 is a print publication proje
derived from the WWP. It offers lightly-annotated versions based o
single good copies or, in some cases, collated versions of texts wit

ore complex editorial histories, normally in their original spelling.
he editions are aimed at a wide audience, from the informed under-
aduate through professional students of literature, and they attempt
 include the general reader who is interested in exploring a fuller tra-
tion of early texts in English than has been available through the
most exclusively male canonical tradition.

SUSANNE WOODS

ELIZABETH H. HAGEMAN

General Editors

ACKNOWLEDGMENTS

The collaborative effort that is the Women Writers Project thrives the contributions of all its members. Ongoing thanks are due to Brov University and its administrators, especially President Vartan Gregoria Provost Frank Rothman, Dean of the Faculty Bryan Shepp, and Vi President Brian Hawkins. Members of the Brown English Departmer particularly Elizabeth Kirk, Stephen Foley, and William Keach, ha provided indispensable advice; many thanks to Marilyn Netter for h help in finding the WWP a new director. Gratitude is also owed to D Wolfe, of Brown's Computing and Information Services. At Brow Scholarly Technology Group, Geoffrey Bilder and Elli Mylonas a unfailingly resourceful and obliging in all matters, and Allen Renear i rare source of energy and inspiration.

Working with Oxford University Press is always a pleasure; ma thanks to Elizabeth Maguire for making the Series possible and Claude Conyers for his unlimited patience, his unfailing sense humor, and the laugh that goes with both.

A more committed set of colleagues than the WWP staff is hard imagine. Project Coordinator Maria Fish facilitates all contacts with tl outside world with her unerring knowledge of protocol and her consi erable diplomatic skills. The computer textbase from which this volun was drawn approaches perfection largely through the efforts of Carc Mah and Syd Bauman. I thank Julia Flanders for defining the positic of managing editor and easing me into the very big shoes she l behind. New Director Carol DeBoer-Langworthy deserves thanks f bringing a hearty serving of Midwestern pragmatism into the offic Others who have made this series possible include Elizabeth Adam Anthony Arnove, Rebecca Bailey, Kim Bordner, Susie Castellanos, Pa Caton, Nick Daly, Cathleen Drake, Faye Halpern, Loren Novec Anastasia Porter, Kasturi Ray, Caleb Rounds, and Kristen Whissel.

ELIZABETH TERZAK
Managing Edit

ACKNOWLEDGMENTS

My challenging task of editing these little-known texts was made easier and much more pleasant thanks to assistance from many sources, especially from colleagues and staff associated with the Women Writers Project at Brown University. The general editor Susanne Woods had the wisdom and foresight to launch the entire project of retrieving and publishing on-line and in print five centuries of women's texts. The co-general editor, Elizabeth Hageman, to whom we are all indebted for a series of indispensable bibliographical essays on sixteenth and seventeenth-century women's writing, offered much help and advice at the beginning of my undertaking. My largest and most direct debt is to my Renaissance section editor, Sara Jayne Steen, whose editorial comments and suggestions made the manuscript much better than it was before. Linda Woodbridge's wide-ranging study of the controversy about women throughout the English Renaissance, and Simon Shepherd's modern edition of several defenses of women, including Speght's *Mouzell*, have been continuously suggestive. My introduction draws on materials in my *Writing Women in Jacobean England* (1993), with the gracious permission of the Harvard University Press.

I am grateful for the help of research librarians in many places: the Houghton Library at Harvard, the Beinecke Library at Yale, the Henry E. Huntington Library, the Folger Shakespeare Library, the British Library, the Bodleian Library, the Guildhall Library in London, and the Merton College Library, Oxford. Experts on seventeenth-century hands at the Beinecke and Houghton Libraries helped me decipher some nearly unreadable words in the marginalia of the Yale *Mouzell*. The manuscript marginalia in the Yale copy are reproduced here with the permission of the Beinecke Rare Book and Manuscript Library, Yale University.

Several people helped me track down some hard-to-find references: Gwynne Blakemore Evans, Sheila ffolliott, Sara Jayne Steen, Violet Halpert, Andrea Sununu, Keith Nightenhelser, and Mary Thomas Crane. Susan Thornberg read proof with exemplary care and attention.

I am also grateful to the Harvard Seminar on Early Modern Women, the 1994 Conference at Dearborn, Michigan, on "Representi Women in Renaissance England," and to my graduate and undergrad ate seminars at Harvard on "Contextualizing Renaissance Women Writing" for discussing some of these materials with me.

This book is dedicated to my husband and my son, who contribu continuously and immeasurably to all my projects.

BARBARA KIEFER LEWALSI

INTRODUCTION

achel Speght, a well-educated young woman of the London middle
ass, is the first Englishwoman to identify herself, by name, as a polem-
st and critic of contemporary gender ideology.[1] Her tract defending
omen, *A Mouzell for Melastomus* (1617),[2] is the first, and may be the
ly, female contribution to the vigorous Jacobean pamphlet war over
omen's place and role. She also claimed the role of poet, publishing in
521 a long poetic meditation on death, *Mortalities Memorandum*,[3]
gether with an allegorical dream-vision poem, *A Dreame*, that
counts her own rapturous encounter with learning and defends
omen's education.

Biographical information about Speght is scarce, as it is for most
her early modern women writers. She was born about 1597 into a
ligious and bourgeois family. Her father, James Speght, was a Calvin-
t minister and the rector of two London churches, St. Mary
lagdalene, Milk Street (1592–1637), and St. Clement, Eastcheap
611–1637).[4] He was also an author and had some associations with
e City establishment. In 1613 he published a tract arguing the Cal-
nist positions on justifying faith and the final perseverance of the
lect, based on the classic proof texts in Romans 8. It is dedicated "To

---

We cannot be sure on present evidence whether a woman wrote the earlier tract entitled
ne Anger her Protection for Women (London, 1589), or if so, who she is. The poet Aemelia
nyer offered a brief defense of women in the epistle "To the Virtuous Reader," in *Salve Deus
x Judaeorum* (1611), ed. Susanne Woods (New York: Oxford University Press, 1993), 48–
.

See title page, page 1, and textual introduction.

See title page, page 43, and textual introduction.

There is no record of Rachel's baptism among the numerous Speght entries in *The Registers
St. Mary Magdalen, Milk Street 1558–1666* (Guildhall microfilm 6984), transcribed by A.
. Hughes Clarke, 2 vols. (London: Harleian Society, 1942). The entries for baptisms,
arriages, and deaths dating back to 1558 are subscribed "per me Jacobum Speght sacrae
eologiae Baccalaurum," suggesting that Rachel's father transcribed those records. It seems
ely that Rachel was baptized in a nearby city church, but the records of most City of London
urches were destroyed in the Great Fire of 1666. Her birthdate is calculated on the basis of
r statement that she had "not yet seen twenty years" when she wrote the *Mouzell* in 1616 and
om her recorded age (twenty-four) at her marriage in 1621.

the Right Worshipful Knights, and Aldermen, to the Wardens a
Assistants of the Society of Goldsmiths" in testimony of their "ki
linking of me in brotherhood," indicating that he was incorporated i
that London guild.[5] On 6 January 1611 he preached before the L
Mayor and aldermen of London an Epiphany sermon on Christ as
Christian's only salvation. He published it in 1615[6] with a dedication
the London alderman who appointed him to deliver it— "To the Rig
Worshipfull Sir Baptiste Hicks, Knight, the Lady Elizabeth his Wi
and to their vertuous of-spring"—identifying the Hicks family as lor
time parishioners, friends, and patrons at St. Mary Magdalen.

Rachel intimates that her mother exercised a profound influence
her life, and states that her death was the stimulus for *Mortalities Me
orandum*. Neither Rachel nor any surviving record provides t
mother's name, dates of birth, marriage, or death, or other biographi
facts, but *A Dreame* indicates that she died after Rachel completed t
Mouzell (registered with the Stationers on 14 November 1616), a
shortly before she wrote *Mortalities Memorandum* (registered on 18 Ja
uary 1621). On 13 February 1621[7] her father remarried. There are
birth or baptismal records of siblings. Thomas Speght, the editor
Chaucer (1598, 1602), may have been a kinsman.

Speght's writings both claim and display a knowledge of Latin a
some training in logic and rhetoric—a classical education very rare f
seventeenth-century women of any class. She cites a wide range
learned authorities in her writings, most of them probably drawn fro
one or more of the numerous popular anthologies or commonpla
books of maxims and sayings that juxtapose classical and Christi

---

5. *A Briefe Demonstration, who have, and of the certainty of their salvation, that have the Spiri
Christ. Published at the instant desire of some godly affected, for the setling of their hope, that
shaken with temptations* (London, 1613).

6. *The Day-spring of Comfort. A Sermon Preached before the Lord Maior and Aldermen
London on Sunday the 6. of January, Anno 1610* [1611] *being also the Feast of Epipha
(London, 1615); reprinted as *The Christian's Comfort. A Sermon Preached before the Lord Ma
and Aldermen of London* (London, 1616).

7. *The Register of St. Clement, Eastcheap*, transcribed by A. W. Hughes Clarke, 2 vols. (Lond
Harleian Society, 1937), 1: 87, records the marriage of "Mr. James Speght, parson of this pari
& Elizabeth Smyth, widdow, of Newington Butts" on 13 February 1621.

urces.[8] Writers of all sorts relied on such collections, sometimes sup-
ementing them from their own commonplace books, as Speght may
ave done. It appears that she also read some history, geography, and
ature lore, parts at least of some classical texts (Plutarch, Cicero, Vir-
l), some vernacular literature, and many sermons, biblical commen-
ries, and manuals of devotion. Like most male grammar-school
udents, she learned her logic and rhetoric from handbooks, not
rectly from Ramus or Aristotle's *Organon,* which she admits she had
ot "so much as seene (though heard of)."[9]

The allegory of *A Dreame* suggests that Speght encountered and
vercame many obstacles in her pursuit of learning—her own fears, the
ssuasions of others, the distractions of domestic duties. It recounts as
ell her delight in learning, and the fact that some unspecified "occur-
ance" forced her, regretfully, to end her studies, to return "to that
lace.../ From whence I came," and to use her time "other-wayes" (ll.
38–40)—presumably in domestic offices. Whatever its scope, her
nusual classical education must have been approved by her father. It
ay have been conducted or supervised by him, or the "return" to her
lace may imply that she was educated elsewhere, possibly in one of the
w schools for young gentlewomen. Also, her father evidently
pproved (and may have encouraged) her answer to Swetnam, since she
rote it while under his authority and does not hint of any difficulties
doing so.

The Moundfords may also have influenced Speght's education, aspi-
ations, and sense of self. *Mortalities Memorandum* is dedicated to her
odmother Mary Moundford, "as a testimonie of my true thankeful-
esse for your fruitfull love, ever since my beeing, manifested toward
e" (page 46 in the present edition). Mary was the wife of Thomas

---

Such books include Francis Meres, *Palladis Tamia* (London, 1598); Nicholas Ling,
oliteuphuia, *Wit's Commonwealth* (London, 1597), both often reprinted; also Robert Allott,
Wit's Theater of the Little World (London, 1599), and William Wrednot's *Palladis Palatium*
London, 1604). I have examined these and several other such works, but was unable to
scover the particular one or ones she used; they may not have survived. I am grateful to Mary
rane for examining the citations and suggesting places to look.

Certaine Quæres, page 37. Given this fact, the mistake noted in the Errata list (*Arganox* for
Organon) was likely hers, not the typesetter's.

Moundford, a renowned London physician who was president six tim¦ of the College of Physicians. The Moundfords lived in Milk Stre¦ neighbors and parishioners of James Speght.[10] Doctor Moundford w¦ also a writer: his Latin tract *Vir Bonus* (1622) carried dedications King James I, to the Bishop of London, and to four judges—an indic¦ tion of his circle of acquaintance.[11] He was physician to several cou¦ notables, among them Arbella Stuart, cousin to King James and impri¦ oned by him for contracting a forbidden marriage that strengthened h¦ claim to the throne. Moundford made himself a partisan of t¦ famously learned Arbella,[12] and that relationship might have led him ¦ encourage the good education of his wife's goddaughter, or at lea¦ directed Rachel's attention to Arbella as a model of female intellectu¦ accomplishments.

The immediate stimulus to Speght's writing was the publication ¦ 1615 of an anonymous attack on women, the rambling, boisterou¦ tonally confused but lively *Araignment of Lewde, idle, froward, an¦ unconstant women.* In the first printing the title page carried no nam¦ and the epistolary preface was signed "Thomas Tel-troth"; Speght's tra¦ claims the exploit of unmasking the author as one Joseph Swetnam, fencing-master.[13] Swetnam's tract inaugurates the rancorous Jacobea¦ skirmish in the centuries-old *querelle des femmes,* or debate over t¦

---

10. *DNB.* The Moundford family is conspicuous in the parish records of St. Mary Magdale¦ "Mr Doctor Moundeford, Phitision" was buried in the church on 13 December 1630, his wi¦ on 9 November 1655.

11. *Vir Bonus* (London, 1622) treats the cardinal virtues of Temperance, Prudence, Fortitud¦ and Justice, emphasizing how Moundford's experience as a doctor has fitted him to comme¦ on the conduct of life. The first impression carries a dedication to James alone; the next (al¦ 1622) adds the other dedicatees. The judges are Sir James Lee, Sir Julius Caesar, Sir Hen¦ Hobart, and Sir Lawrence Tanfield. Earlier, Moundford translated from French into Lat¦ André de Laurens, *De Morbis Melancholis, & eorum cura Tractatus* (London, 1599).

12. He colluded with her efforts to prevent exile to Durham by pleading illness, interceded f¦ her with James, and was briefly imprisoned on suspicion of aiding her escape to France wi¦ her husband. For her life and learning see Lewalski, *Writing Women,* 67–92, and Sara Jayr¦ Steen's introduction to her edition of Arbella's *Letters* (New York: Oxford University Pres¦ 1994).

13. Thomas Tel-troth [Joseph Swetnam], *The Araignment of Lewde, idle, froward, ar¦ unconstant women: Or the vanitie of them, choose you whether* (London: E. Allde for T. Arche¦ 1615). The tract was entered into the Stationers' Register 8 February 1615. In later edition¦ his cover blown, Swetnam signed his epistle with his full name. His only other known boc¦ deals with fencing, *The Schoole of the Noble and Worthy Science of Defence* (London, 1617).

ture and worth of womankind. His prefatory epistles seem deliber-
:ly calculated to provoke responses from women or their defenders,
gesting an effort by the author and the bookseller, Thomas Archer,
start a profitable controversy.

Two years later (1617) the same bookseller published *A Mouzell*
uzzle] *for Melastomus* [black mouth], naming Rachel Speght as
thor on the title page. We can only speculate about the circumstances
at elicited this reply at this juncture. Speght herself may have decided
answer Swetnam and then presented her tract to Swetnam's book-
ller, Archer. More likely, however, she was solicited by Archer to write
is rejoinder in an effort to reawaken the controversy two years later
d sell more books. If so, she must have been suggested to him by fam-
 or friends, or else, at age nineteen, she had already acquired some
putation in city circles as a learned young woman. She seeks patron-
e as male writers customarily do, but targets female patrons, dedicat-
g her tract "To all vertuous Ladies Honourable or Worshipfull"
oblewomen and wives of city officials]. Pointing to her special vulner-
ility as a young woman writer, she asserts that the danger of her enter-
ise requires her to "impetrate patronage from some of power"
age 5).

Of the eight major contributors to the Swetnam and cross-dressing
ntroversies of 1615–1620 only Speght published under her own
ame and indeed insisted on her authorial identity.[14] Later in 1617 two
her answers to Swetnam under female pseudonyms were published by
ifferent booksellers—Nicholas Bourne and Lawrence Hayes—who
idently wanted to get in on a lucrative controversy and keep it going.
he writers may be women, or (perhaps more likely) men strategically
presenting themselves as women rushing to improve upon Speght's
swer to Swetnam. These tracts offer very different estimations of
peght. In *Ester hath hang'd Haman* Ester Sowernam (punning on
we[e]tnam) condescends to Speght, adopting the persona of a mature,
perienced woman who somehow has escaped all the usual catego-

---

. Swetnam's tract and the other two answers to it (discussed below) were published
eudonymously; a stage play dealing with the controversy was anonymous, as were the three
acts published in 1620 on the related issue of cross-dressing—*Hic Mulier: or, the Man-*
oman; Haec Vir: or, The Womanish Man; and *Muld Sacke: Or the Apologie of Hic Mulier.*

ries—"neither Maide, Wife nor Widdowe, yet really all, and therefo
experienced to defend all."[15] She justifies writing her tract by referri
to the inadequate answers of the young and inexperienced "mai
whom she also knows to be a "ministers daughter": "I did observe, th
whereas the Maide doth many times excuse her tendernesse of yeares
found it to be true in the slendernesse of her answer, for she underta
ing to defend women, doth rather charge and condemne women."[16]
contrast, in *The Worming of a mad Dogge,* Constantia Munda prais
Speght's achievement, explaining that she wrote her own tract befo
Speght's appeared, and is publishing it now because Swetnam is offeri
to growl back at Speght:

> You see your blacke grinning mouth hath been muzled by a modest and
> powerfull hand, who hath judiciously bewrayed, and wisely layed open
> your singular ignorance, couched under incredible impudence, who hath
> most gravely (to speake in your owne language) *unfoulded every pleat, and
> shewed every rinckle* of a prophane and brutish disposition, so that tis a
> doubt whether shee hath shewed more modesty or gravity, more learning
> or prudence in the religious confutation of your undecent raylings. But
> as shee hath been the first Champion of our sexe that would encounter
> with the barbarous bloudhound, and wisely damned up your mouth, and
> sealed up your jawes lest your venomed teeth like madde dogges should
> damage the credit of many, nay all innocent damosels...I heare you
> foame at mouth and groule against the Author with another head like the
> triple dog of hell; wherefore I have provided this sop for *Cerberus.*[17]

See the appendix in the present volume for what may be Swetnam
annotations on a copy of Speght's tract in preparation for that grow
ing answer.

Speght's treatise received other public notice. Her title *Melastom*
was used to taunt Swetnam in an anonymous comedy (perhaps

---

15. Ester Sowernam, *Ester hath hang'd Haman: or, An Answere to a lewd Pamphlet, entituled T
Arraignment of Women. with the arraignment of lewd, idle, froward, and unconstant men, a
Husbands. Divided into two Parts. The first presents the dignity and worthinesse of Women, ou
divine Testimonies. The second shewing the estimation of the Foeminine Sexe, in ancient and Pag
times* (London, 1617). Sowernam's self-description is on the title page.

16. *Ibid.,* sig. A2v. The comment that Speght charges and condemns women is unjustifi
she merely makes the usual distinction between good and bad women to underscore Swetnar
failure to fulfill his promise to do so, insisting that there are good and bad of both sexes.

17. Constantia Munda, *The Worming of a mad Dogge: Or, a Soppe for Cerberus the Jaylor
Hell. No Confutation but a sharpe Redargation of the bayter of Women* (London, 1617), 16.

homas Heywood), *Swetnam the Woman-hater Arraigned by Women.*
roduced in 1618 or 1619 and published in 1620, it ends with a court
ene in which women reveal Swetnam's identity, convict him, muzzle
id torment him. A resumé of Swetnam's history contains a pun on
achel's name:

> He put his Booke i' the Presse, and publisht it,
> And made a thousand men and wives fall out.
> Till two or three good wenches, in meere spight [speght],
> Laid their heads together, and rail'd him out of th' Land.[18]

a the epistle to the poems she published in 1621, Speght refers to the
ariety of comments her tract provoked. She exhibits considerable equa-
imity in the face of criticism, but rises to answer those who (refusing
credit female achievement) have attributed her tract to her father,
ffering her poems as, in part, a gesture to reassert her authorial rights:

> I know these populous times affoord plentie of forward Writers, and
> criticall Readers; My selfe hath made the number of the one too many by
> one; and having bin toucht with the censures of the other, by occasion of
> my *mouzeling Melastomus,* I am now, as by a strong motive induced (for
> my rights sake) to produce and divulge this off-spring of my indevour, to
> prove them further futurely who have formerly deprived me of my due,
> imposing my abortive upon the father of me, but not of it. Their variety
> of verdicts have verified the adagie *quot homines, tot sententiae* [there are
> as many opinions as there are men] and made my experience confirme
> that apothegme which doth affirme Censure to be inevitable to a
> publique act (page 45).

Ier epistle disposes briskly of gender constraints on publication by
ppealing to unimpeachable religious motives—the desire to benefit
chers by leading them to prepare for death, and the biblical command
› use and not hide a God-given talent:

> Amongst diversitie of motives to induce the divulging of that to publique
> view, which was devoted to private Contemplation, none is worthy to
> precede desire of common benefit. Corne kept close in a garner feeds not
> the hungry; A candle put under a bushell doth not illuminate an house;

---

8. *Swetnam the Woman-hater. Arraigned by Women. A new Comedie, Acted at the Red Bull by
·e late Queenes Servants* (London, 1620), sig. I4v.

None but unprofitable servants knit up Gods talent in a Napkin. These premises have caused the Printing presse to expresse the subsequent *Memorandum of Mortalitie* (page 45).

The curiously passive terms of this rationale intimate that these go motives caused the printing press to operate apart from Speght's ov actions. But this is less female self-effacement than it is a modest way f Speght to position herself among those whose talents must not wasted and whose private thoughts are able to benefit others. The fo mula may also imply some initiative from the bookseller—Jacc Bloome this time, not Archer. Her epistle indicates that this Lond gentlewoman was not much troubled by the anxieties about authorsh and publication common among the upper classes, and especial women. She may indeed have hoped to earn money from writing as quasi-professional author.

Speght's later life is a virtual blank. On 2 August 1621, a license w issued for the marriage of "Procter, William, gent ["clerk," i.e., cleric, the vicar-general's book], bachelor, 29, and Rachel Speight, spinster, 2 daughter of Mr. James Speight, clerk, parson of St. Mary Magdale Milk Street, London, who consents."[19] On 6 August the marriage w performed at St. Mary Woolchurch haw, London. It is not obvious wl this choice, rather than her father's church or St. Botolph's Aldersgat identified as her own and William Procter's parish church.[20] All thr churches were within a few blocks of each other. The phrase indicatir paternal consent often meant that the couple had a special license di pensing with the three-week reading of the bans.

Rachel's husband was probably the "Procter, William of Somers (plebs)" who matriculated at Oriel College in October 1609 at age si teen.[21] There are many Procters and Proctors (though no William)

---

19. Joseph Foster, ed., *London Marriage Licences, 1521–1869* (London, 1887), 1098.

20. On 6 August the marriage is registered between "Mr. William Proctor and Rachel Spigl both of St. Buttals [Botolph's] Aldersgate," in the parish records of St. Mary Woolchurch ha (Guildhall, microfilm 7644), transcribed by J. M. S. Brooke and A. H. Hallen, *The Transcr of the Records of the United Parishes of S. Mary Woolnoth and S. Mary Woolchurch haw* (Londo 1886), 351.

21. *Alumni Oxoniensis*, ed. Joseph Foster (Oxford, 1891), 3:1215.

e parish records of St. Mary Magdalen, including the churchwarden
:ob Proctor who regularly signed the register entries. It seems likely
at this was a marriage arranged between closely allied families, provid-
ʒ Rachel with a minister husband akin to her father in his Calvinist
eology and City connections. In 1624 the Procters were probably liv-
ʒ at Upminster in Essex, just outside London, from which place one
illiam Procter (almost certainly the same man) dated his publication,
ʒe *Watchman Warning,* dedicating it to the "Right Worshipfull Master
ılph Freeman, Alderman."[22] This Calvinist sermon was first preached
Paul's Cross on 26 September 1624 and addressed to the "whole
onorable Corporation" of City officers. Baptismal records of two chil-
en, Rachel (26 February 1627) and William (15 December 1630) at
, Giles, Cripplegate, specify that their father, William Procter, is a
inister and indicate that the family then lived in that parish.[23] As
ese children bear their parents' names, they were probably the first
ʼo born alive; I found no record of other children or of Rachel
•eght's death and burial.[24] Her father died in 1637.[25] William Procter
ed in 1653 and was buried at All Hallows, Lombard Street.[26]

, William Procter, *The Watchman Warning. A Sermon Preached at Pauls Crosse the 26. of
›tembere, 1624* (London, 1625). Procter identifies himself as "Master of Arts and Minister of
·ds Word," dating his preface "From my house at Upminster in Essex, this 20 of October,
24." The sermon is offered as a "forewarning of this famous Citie especially, and the whole
·gdome also," who are inviting destruction for their sins. It develops the metaphor of
nisters as watchmen, and justifies God's decree of reprobation against sinners.

. The parish registers of St. Giles, Cripplegate (Guildhall, microfilm 6419/2) record these
›tisms: "Rachell dau: of William Procter Minister" (26 February 1626 [1627]; and
/illiam, sonne of Mr. William Procter Minister" (15 December 1630). The mother's name is
t given (in parish records it sometimes is and sometimes is not).

. The Guildhall burial index, 1538–1853, records only men's burials. Parish records
ʒularly enter women's burials, but for the period in question the records for most City
urches were destroyed by the Great Fire of 1666. Since there is no record in Foster, *London
arriage Licences,* of a license issued for a second Procter marriage, Rachel evidently died
›metime after her son William's birth (1630) and may have survived her husband.

. The parish records of St. Mary Magdalen, Milk Street (Guildhall, microfilm 4783) record
e burial "within the Rail" on 7 April 1637, of "James Speght, Doctor in Divinity and Rector
this Parish." This meant he was buried in the area close to the altar, set off from the nave of
e church by the communion rail.

. Parish registers of All Hallows, Lombard Street (Guildhall, microfilm 17,614) record the
rial of one William Proctor in 1653.

A Mouzell for Melastomus (1617)

The extended context for Speght's treatise is the centuries-old deb:
over the nature and worth of womankind, the so-called *querelle .*
femmes. Some defenses of women, especially that of Christine de Pis:
challenged misogynist stereotypes, offering positive images of fem:
warriors, rulers, and scholars and exposing male bias and interest
subjugating women.[27] But as Linda Woodbridge shows, throughc
the English Renaissance the formal polemic controversy over wom:
owed more to rhetorical convention than to ideological conviction
emotional involvement.[28] In substance, these tracts and other te:
recycled hoary arguments pro and con; in form, they relied heavily ·
the judicial oration and the outrageous paradox. Most of the writ:
were participants in an on-going game of wit played by men for th:
own and (they seem to have supposed) women's amusement.

The immediate context for Swetnam's tract and Speght's answer
the apparent challenge to gender hierarchy in the oppositional writin:
and activities of some Jacobean women, including Queen Anne.[29] O:
such gesture was the fad of female cross-dressing, adopted by high-bo:
ladies as well as by such legendary lower-class roaring girls as Long M:
of Westminster and Moll Cutpurse. Thomas Adams wrote in 1615 th:
it was becoming difficult to tell men from women on the streets of Lo:
don, "for the *Amazons* beare away the Bell,"[30] and early in 1620 Ki:
James urged the clergy "to inveigh vehemently and bitterly in theyre s:

---

27. Christine de Pisan (1364–1430), *The Boke of the Cyte of Ladys,* trans. Brian Ans:
(London, 1521). Another very influential though perhaps ironic defense of women :
Heinrich Cornelius Agrippa's *De Nobilitate et Praecellentia Foemenei Sexus,* in *Opera* (Lyo
1531), trans. David Clapham, *A Treatise of the Nobilitie and excellencye of women kyr*
(London, 1542).

28. Linda Woodbridge, *Women and the English Renaissance: Literature and the Nature*
Womankind, 1540–1620 (Urbana: University of Illinois Press, 1984).

29. For Queen Anne's masques and the oppositional writings of some contemporaries :
Lewalski, *Writing Women in Jacobean England* (Cambridge: Harvard University Press, 199
Aemelia Lanyer's *Salve Deus Rex Judaeorum* (1611) contains a brief formal defense of wom:
and the entire volume of poetry praises women and implies their moral and spirit:
superiority to men (see the edition by Susanne Woods).

30. Thomas Adams, *Mystical Bedlam. Or the World of Mad-Men* (London, 1615), 50.

ons against the insolencie of our women, and theyre wearing of brode
imd hats, pointed dublets, theyre haire cut short or shorne, and some
˙ them stillettaes or poinards, and such other trinckets of like
oment."[31] Numerous ballads, sermons, and tracts prompted by the
omen's rebellious gestures made the "woman question" a prominent
cus of interest and anxiety during James's second decade.

Swetnam's tract thus seized an opportune moment. His work is a
.mble of proverb lore, rowdy jokes, invective, authorities, anecdotes
ıd examples pertaining to women's lechery, vanity, shrewishness, and
orthlessness, cobbled together from the entire tradition of misogynist
riting. Swetnam says he expects to be "bitten" by women, who will go
»out to "reprove" his book, but warns them not to answer lest they
:veal their "galled backs to the world"; and he threatens women with a
:t fiercer "second booke, which is almost ready." Such remarks,
»gether with his disclaimer that "I wrote this booke with my hand, but
ot with my heart...my mouth hath uttered that in my fury, which my
eart never thought" and his advice to those already involved with
·omen to "esteeme of this booke onely as the toyes of an idle head," sig-
al that he is writing in the spirit of the rhetorical game.[32] Swetnam
:eeded no second book: this one proved popular enough to go through
:n editions by 1634.

Speght's tract breaks the mold of such rhetorical gamesmanship,
;chewing many of the tired formulaic gestures of the *querelle*
:efenses.[33] Instead, she undertakes to re-interpret biblical texts so as to
1ake the dominant discourse—Protestant biblical exegesis—yield a
1ore expansive and equitable concept of gender. She devises a structure
1at allows her to attack Swetnam on particular points (as the genre and
:adership of such polemics required) but also to develop her own argu-
1ent. Her sometimes trenchant invective against Swetnam's logic and

1. Reported by John Chamberlain, *Letters*, ed. N. E. McClure, 3 vols. (Philadelphia:
merican Philosophical Society, 1939), 2:286–87, 289.

2. Swetnam, *Arraignment*, sigs. A2v–A4, p. 64.

3. Such as citing lists of good women to balance the evil examples adduced, citing authorities
ho praise women to counter the defamers, and overstating claims for female superiority to
»unter outrageous claims for male superiority.

style is restricted to her prefatory matter and poems, and to appended small tract, *Certaine Quaeres to the bayter of Women,* with separate title page, epistle, and preface. In the *Mouzell* proper she virt ally ignores Swetnam in order to mount a serious, coherent, liberalizi critique of gender ideology. By her extended examination of the C ation-Fall story from Genesis and other biblical texts (supported many cross-references in the margins in the approved manner of Prot tant theological argument) Speght looks past Swetnam to engage w thier antagonists—all those ministers or other commentators who fi in scripture some basis to devalue and wholly subjugate women.

While her dedicatory epistle invites patronage from women of ra and power, it also reaches out to all virtuous and god-fearing women every station, "rich and poore, learned and unlearned" (page 4), inviti them to see themselves as the common target of the malevolent Sw nam. Here and elsewhere she comes close to recognizing the comm plight of all *"Hevahs* sex" (page 4) as an oppressed gender in a misog nist, patriarchal society, though she offers herself as the defender not all women but of all good women.

Throughout, Speght mounts an effective answer to Swetnam by cr ating a persona who is the living refutation of Swetnam's charges again women. She presents herself as religious, learned, serious, truthful, em nently rational, engagingly modest, unassuming, justifiably angry y self-controlled, and courageous in defending wronged women and the Creator. She modestly admits her youthful and female insufficiencies learning—"I am young in yeares, and more defective in knowledge, th little smattering in Learning which I have obtained, being only the fru of such vacant houres, as I could spare from affaires befitting my Se (page 31). But she counters this modesty topos by displaying her capa ity for logical argument, her knowledge of rhetoric, her ease with Lat quotations and wordplay (it may be "small Latin" but she seems in to erably good control of it), and her range of reference beyond the Bib to the church fathers and some classical authors: Lactantius, Senec Aristotle, Zoilus, Livy, Pliny, Cicero, Augustine, Plutarch. She also tak pride in her ability to manage a syllogism. Though she has not studi the famous logicians directly, she can do a better syllogism than Swe nam and one that proves him damnable: "To fasten a lie upon God asphemy: But the *Bayter of women* fastens a lie upon God [in falsely aiming that God called women necessary evils]: *ergo,* the *Bayter* is a asphemer" (page 37). Speght appears to accept without demur the ays in which gender has restricted her access to learning, but that ceptance holds a quite subversive subtext: if Rachel's "vacant houres" study have made her so much more learned than Swetnam with all s supposed masculine advantages, then her example makes the case women's equal intelligence and equal capacity for education.[34] Against this persona she poses her character of Swetnam based on his ct: "the very embleme of a monster" (page 4), a blustering, scandal-ongering, indeed blasphemous bully who is *"Irreligious and Illiterate"* age 1), whose grammatical faults and stylistic errors reveal his abys-al ignorance, and whose disjointed and contradictory arguments veal his intellectual, moral, and spiritual chaos. Her governing meta-or for her encounter with him is unequal combat, a David battling oliath, or a St. George with the Dragon. She is "yong, and the unwor-iest of thousands" doing battle with a "furious enemy to our sexe" age 3); she ventures to "fling this stone at vaunting *Goliah"*; she is arless because "armed with the truth" and the "Word of Gods Spirit" age 4).

Many of Speght's arguments in the *Mouzell* proper are common-aces of liberal Protestant marriage doctrine and earlier defenses of omen, but they have considerable subversive potential in pressing the blical/Christian discourse to affirm categorically the moral and spiri-al equality of women, thereby removing any essential ground for omen's subordination to men. And while she admits, as she has to, ose biblical texts proclaiming woman the "weaker vessel" (1 Pet. 3:7) d the man the "head" of the wife in marriage (1 Cor. 11:3), she point-lly refrains from justifying that headship on the usual ground of

---

. In his fencing manual (1617) Swetnam is at pains to insist on his limited formal ucation: "I was never at *Oxford* but while I baited my horse; nor at *Cambridge* but while one urbridge faire lasted"; "I am no Scholler, for I do protest I never went to Schoole six moneths all my life" (sig. A4, p. 195). This may be an effort to deflect Speght's taunts. As Swetnam's anual is not listed in the Stationers' Register we cannot be sure that it postdates Speght's, but at is likely since Speght's was listed in the Stationers' Register on 14 November 1616.

woman's natural inferiority, spelled out in detail in the officially p
mulgated "Homily of the State of Matrimony":

> For the woman is a weake creature, not indued with like strength and
> constancy of minde, therefore, they bee the sooner disquieted, and they
> bee the more prone to all weake affections and dispositions of minde,
> more then men bee, and lighter they bee, and more vaine in their fantisies
> and opinions....The woman ought to have a certain honour attributed
> to her, that is to say, shee must bee spared and borne with, the rather for
> that she is the weaker vessel, of a frail heart inconstant, and with a word
> soon stirred to wrath....To obey, is an other thing then to controle or
> command, which yet they [women] may doe, to their children, and to
> their family: but as for their husbandes, them they must obey, and cease
> from commanding, and performe subjection....By the apparell of her
> head...is signified, that she is under covert or obedience of her
> husband.[35]

The principle of natural female inferiority is reiterated constantly
contemporary marriage sermons and tracts: the wife must obey her hu
band "because he is her better"; the wife must "acknowledge her infe
orities" and "carry her selfe as an inferior"; the husband is "as it were
little God in the family."[36] By contrast, Speght subjects the term "hea
to an exegesis which removes every sanction for the husband's authori
from female nature itself, as created or as redeemed. Gender hierarchy
made to seem simply a somewhat anomalous social institution san
tioned in the Bible primarily to afford protection to women's compar
tive physical weakness. Moreover, Speght defies the often-articulat
precept that wives owe total obedience even to evil husbands (unle
they are infidels)[37] by appealing to the central tenet of Protestantism-
the primacy of the individual conscience.

Speght grounds her central proposition of woman's excellence in t
Genesis story of woman as God's gift to man, and in Aristotle's fo
causes. The efficient cause of woman's creation is God himself, and

---

35. "A Homilie of the State of Matrimonie," in *The Seconde Tome of Homilies* (London, 159
These official homilies were appointed to be read regularly in the churches during Elizabe
reign, and the practice continued under James.

36. Henry Smith, *A Preparative to Marriage* (London, 1591), 62; William Whately, *A Bri
Bush: Or, A Direction for Married Persons* (London, 1616), 189, 113.

37. See, e.g., William Gouge, *Of Domesticall Duties: Eight Treatises* (London, 1622), 317–1

e work "can not chuse but be good, yea very good" (page 18). The
aterial cause, Adam's rib, is more refined matter than the dust from
hich Adam himself was made. The formal cause shapes both man and
oman after the image of God, and Speght elides the usual qualifica-
ɔns about women's supposedly cold humors or imperfect bodies:

> For as God gave man a lofty countenance, that hee might looke up
> toward Heaven, so did he likewise give unto woman. And as the
> temperature of mans body is excellent, so is womans....And (that more
> is) in the Image of God were they both created (page 19).

Ĵoman's final cause or purpose is to glorify God and give good counsel
ɑd companionship to her husband.

Speght concludes that "God...makes their authority equall, and all
ʿeatures to be in subjection unto them both" (page 18). She also emp-
es problematic biblical texts of damaging significance for women. The
ory of the Fall reveals Eve's good intentions and Adam's greater guilt.
ɑul's statement (1 Cor. 7:1) that "it is good for a man not to touch a
ʿoman" refers only to the times and conditions of persecution—an
npressive and potentially radical claim that culture and historical cir-
ɪmstances are determinants even of sacred texts. Similarly, Solomon's
atement (Eccles. 7:30) that he has not found an upright woman
ɲong a thousand refers only to his own guilty association with his
ɪousand pagan concubines.

Her most radical claims are extrapolations from Galatians 3:28, that
nder the New Testament *male and female are all one in Christ Jesus*
ɔage 16). Accordingly, she applies the parable of the talents to women,
ɪferring that "no power externall or internall ought woman to keep
lle, but to imploy it in some service of GOD" (page 20); and her own
ɔt of writing this tract makes the case that some talents ask employ-
ɲent beyond the domestic sphere. She also challenges the pervasive for-
ɲula in treatises on marital duties and in Swetnam that defines separate
ɔheres for men and women[38] by citing examples from nature—
ɪgeons, cocks and hens—that exhibit mates sharing all the offices and

---

3. See, e.g., Robert Cleaver, *A Godlie Forme of Household Government* (London, 1598), 170:
The dutie of the husband is, to travell abroad to seeke living: and the wives dutie is to keep the
ɔuse"; and Whately, *Bride-Bush,* 84: "He without doores, she within: he abroad, she at
ɔme."

duties of life. She often celebrates marriage as an estate far more exce lent than the single life, invoking the familar pun, "merri-age." Her ep logue concludes with a stern warning: Men who speak and write again women are guilty of that most odious vice, ingratitude toward God, a invite God's certain revenge for reviling his best gift and handiwo "women I meane, whom God hath made equall with themselves in di nity, both temporally and eternally" (page 26).

The other parts of the volume are chiefly in the satiric mode. T preface inaugurates a double-pronged attack on Swetnam as both illite ate and irreligious, and shows Speght devising a railing style that sometimes witty, occasionally heavy-handed. By his own bear-baitir metaphor Swetnam has labelled himself a dog (and thereby a cynic Latin). He uses "such irregularities touching concordance" and "so di ordered a methode" that a mere grammar-school student could cat him out (page 7). His tract is altogether "without methode…a promi cuous mingle mangle" (page 31). His failures in logic match those grammar as he draws absurd conclusions and often contradicts himsel Moreover, he has put himself beyond the pale of Christianity: he bla phemes God by wresting and perverting scripture; he disparag woman, "that excellent worke of Gods hands"; and he looks to "he thenish" authorities for his misogynist ideas (page 8). Three commer datory poems under the names "Philalethes," "Favour B," an "Philomathes," probably by Rachel herself,[39] reinforce her youthf achievement and the David/St. George analogues. A witty acrost poem on Swetnam's name signed by Speght unmasks him and furth displays her talents.

In *Certaine Quaeres* Speght instances specific examples of Swetnam grammatical errors and illogic, spicing them with invective and pun He counts womens' changes of mood *"Wonderfull"* but she thinks hir "farre more *wonder-foole"* for his failures in grammatical concordance– for example, joining *"Women* plural and *shee* singular" (page 35). St puns regularly on "as/ass," pointing to Swetnam: "And where-asse yo

---

39. The poem by "Philomathes" contains an unusual Latinism, "obtrectation," that Speg often uses, and the verse in all three poems resembles Speght's in her later poems.

"; "such a monster in nature *Asse* your selfe" (page 34); *"Asse*
u...have done" (page 35). Swetnam cannot recognize the figure of
eech "sarcasmus" in the words of Job's wife; nor the biblical counter-
amples to his generalizations about women's ingratitude and the cru-
y of fair women; nor Ovid's supposed error about the properties of
e. She catches him up also on his occasional repetition of statements
m the defenses of women and marriage which contradict the thrust
his argument. Finally, her refusal to answer Swetnam's attacks on
dows—"in that I am ignorant of their dispositions" (page 40)—con-
ts Swetnam of the highest presumption in daring to comment on
men's lives, with which he has no experience whatever.

Mortalities Memorandum (1621)

eght's second volume provides further insight into her sense of self,
r role as author, and the conditions which empowered her to write
d publish. It is conceived as a tribute to the women most important
her (her recently deceased mother and her godmother), as a religious
nefit to others, and as a means to claim her authorial rights to the
ti-Swetnam tract. The readership of this work is not gendered,
ough the verse address "To the Reader" makes Speght's familiar dis-
iction between the ignorant censorious reader and the *"courteous
ader"* who respects art and *"learnings fruit"* (page 47).

The title poem of *Mortalities Memorandum* both urges, and offers
elf as an example of, a proper Christian meditation on death. The
ief topics are: the origins of death in the Fall; the three kinds of death
entioned in scripture; the benefits death brings to the faithful; the
mparison of this world's pains with heaven's delights; the evils of
man life in this world in all ages, conditions, and stages; the comfort
e godly can find in death; the motives we have to meditate on death;
d finally the special benefits of such meditation. The verse (756 lines,
six-line iambic pentameter stanzas, rhymed *abcbdd*) is generally
distinguished. There are a few sharp images, effective figures, and
resting rhetorical questions, but the poem is replete with religious
mmonplaces, the language is often prosaic, and the rhymes are some-
mes awkward and strained. Speght argues with wit and vigor in prose,

but she evidently found no models like Samuel Daniel's verse epistles
John Davies's *Nosce Teipsum* to teach her how to conduct an effect
moral argument in verse.

Yet the poem is a fascinating cultural document. For one this
Speght offers it as a sanctioned way for a woman to instruct a Christi
audience, thereby claiming a share in the work of her minister fatl
and husband-to-be. Like them, Speght was a Calvinist, as the poe
references to election, reprobation, and to God's "chosen" or "destina
(ll. 15, 24, 44–54) make clear. She also reveals, rather amusingly, l
bourgeois concern with wills and the disposition of property, pointi
to such arrangements as one major benefit of regular meditation
death. Her experience with the market-driven *querelle* controversy n
have prompted her to recognize the large middle-class market for boc
on piety, devotion, and self-analysis[40] as an opportunity for a would-
professional woman writer.

Much more effective on all counts is her prefatory poem, *A Drea*
(50 stanzas, 300 lines), described as substantially autobiographic
"imaginarie in manner, *reall in matter*" (page 43). It uses the san
stanza form, with often pedestrian verse and, initially, some awkwa
poetic diction. But this dream-vision poem is much enlivened by t
allegorical fiction, by the dialogue of the speaker with allegorical chara
ters, by the author's emotional engagement with sensitive autobi
graphical concerns, and especially by the fictional representation of
woman's obstacle-laden path to education. It cleverly plays off roman
a genre long associated with women readers, and especially that clas
of romance literature, the *Romance of the Rose,* whose lover-hero is va
ously hindered by or helped by many personifications of courtly lo
psychology and social custom in his efforts to enter the delicious Ga
den of Love and pluck the budding rose of love. Its numerous versio
and adaptations in medieval and Renaissance literature include a part

---

40. See Louis B. Wright, *Middle-Class Culture in Elizabethan England* (Chapel Hill: Univers
of North Carolina Press, 1935), 228–96.

anslation by Chaucer and Spenser's Temple of Venus (*Faerie Queene*, ook 4, Canto 10).[41]

In Speght's poem Rachel, the speaker, recounts a dream which led er "Into a place most pleasant to the eye" named Cosmos where, vanting wisdom," she finds herself suddenly amazed and disconsoe. Approached by Thought, who inquires the reason for her grief and omises aid, she names her problem as *"Ignorance"*—defined very genally:

> I feele disease, yet know not what I ayle,
> I finde a sore, but can no salve provide;
> I hungry am, yet cannot seeke for food;
> Because I know not what is bad or good (ll. 51–54).

norance has reduced her to a brutish reliance on instinct, and to solipsm: "I measure all mens feet by mine owne shooe" (l. 65). Thought nds her to Age, who directs her to Experience. In her turn, Experience commends Knowledge as "The onely medicine for your maladie," cating it "In *Eruditions* garden" and promising that Industry will serve Rachel's guide (ll. 91, 100). The allegory suggests that some persons f age and experience (Rachel's father? or mother? the Moundfords? her friends?) helped her acquire an education and realize its benefits.

A dialogue follows in which Dissuasion sets forth the many difficules in Rachel's way—"As dulnesse, and my memories defect;/ The diffiltie of attaining lore,/ My time, and sex, with many others more" (ll. 06–8)—and is answered by Desire, Truth, and Industry. Industry romises to "cut away/ All obstacles, that in her way can grow" and preicts victory: "by the issue of her owne attempt,/ I'll make thee *labor mnia vincet* know" (ll. 121–24, labor will conquer all). This allusion to irgil's *Georgics* 1.145, playing off against the romance expectation of he more familiar saying, *"Amor vincit omnia"* (love conquers all), makes oman's province not love but intellectual labor and shows Speght taking considerable credit for her own industry and achievements. Truth

---

. Guillaume de Lorris began the poem around 1237 but left it incomplete; an anonymous et produced a seventy-eight page conclusion; around 1277 Jean de Meun wrote a vast new nplification (21,780 lines) with a quite different emphasis. See *The Romance of the Rose*, trans. arry W. Robbins, ed. Charles W. Dunn (New York: Dutton, 1962).

speaks to the gender issue, claiming that the natures of men and wom
are alike suited to education on precisely the same basis—the equali
of their intellects and the fact that God himself requires from both m
and women the use of all talents. In evidence she cites several classi
examples of learned women (Demophila and Telesilla for poetry, Co
nelia for prose style, Hypatia for astronomy, Aspatia for rhetoric, Are
for art, others for science). Speght chose to omit such examples fro
her biblically-grounded indictment of Swetnam, or perhaps she on
learned of them subsequently, from Plutarch and various commonpla
collections. They are entirely appropriate to this poem's defense
women's general education.

Rachel is then led by Industry to *"Instructions* pleasant ayre" whe
she delights in the "taste of science" and desires to "reape this pleasu
more and more." Wandering with Desire she meets Truth again, wh
delivers a paeon to knowledge, forcefully countering the familiar arg
ments in contemporary tracts for limiting woman's education to what
of practical use in her life: the Bible, religious treatises, grammar, han
writing, domestic skills (and for aristocrats, music, dancing, and mo
ern languages). By those arguments, women are quite properly deni
the classical humanist education intended to prepare young men f
public life. Truth, however, takes the high line that the very nature
humankind makes all knowledge useful for all humans. It is Spegh
most progressive argument, buttressed by numerous scriptural citatio
in the margins (Col. 3:10, Prov. 19:2, John 17:3), and no doubt deriv
its urgency from her own experience in opposing the restrictive view
women's education in her own life:

> ...by it [knowledge] Gods image man doth beare,
> Without it he is but a humane shape,
> Worse then the Devill; for he knoweth much;
> Without it who can any ill escape?
> By vertue of it evils are withstood;
> *The minde without it is not counted good.*
>
> · · · · · · · · · · · · · ·
>
> This true report put edge unto *Desire,*
> Who did incite me to increase my store,

And told me 'twas a lawfull avarice,
To covet *Knowledge* daily more and more.
This counsell I did willingly obey,
Till some occurrence called me away.

And made me rest content with that I had,
Which was but little, as effect doth show;
And quenched hope for gaining any more,
For I my time must other-wayes bestow.
I therefore to that place return'd againe,
From whence I came, and where I must remaine
(ll. 205–10, 229–40).

eght's plaintive report links that "occurrence" to the duties and the
edience demanded of women in the era. She obeys, but makes her
smay evident, indicating that she has not internalized this construc-
n of woman's role.

If, as is likely, the chronology of the allegory conforms to Rachel's
e, shortly after being recalled by the "occurrence" to her own place she
w the "full fed Beast" [Swetnam] attacking women, and was
ompted (in 1616) to muzzle him. She was then nineteen, by which
e her formal education would surely have ended, though she did not
arry until four years later. She also incorporates the allegorical perso-
e of Sowernam and Munda into her allegorical fiction, answering
wernam's condescension by describing her as a "selfe-conceited Crea-
re," but repaying Munda's praises by crediting her tract with effec-
vely stopping Swetnam (ll. 247–64). The stimulus for her second
ok (1621) Speght allegorizes as another monster, an all-devouring
enserian beast (Death) whom she sees in a dream as a "fierce insatiable
e,/Depopulating Countries" (ll. 267–68). When it slays her mother
e is startled awake, and finds the event true. And again, as with Swet-
am, she takes on the role of a courageous romance heroine daring to
counter and seek revenge on a cruel and terrible foe.

In the *Mouzell* Speght does not attack patriarchy as a social arrange-
ent, but she does deny any essential basis for it in nature or in the
iritual order. She also represents the family in terms very different
om those of King James, who saw it as an analogue of the absolutist
ate. Speght's allegorical *Dreame* offers an uncompromising defense of

woman's education on the same basis as man's education; she also rep
sents herself enjoying, and then forced to give over, that pleasure due
some obviously gendered circumstance. Speght's serious effort
rethink the implications of the dominant biblical discourse in regard
women was provoked by Swetnam, but the *Dreame* suggests that it v
also provoked by her own situation as a learned young woman hedg
about by restrictions. Both tract and poem strongly, cogently, and su
versively argue her own and all good women's worth and substan
equality.

TEXTUAL INTRODUCTION

Rachel Speght's quarto volume *A Mouzell for Melastomus* was enter
into the Stationers' Register on 14 November 1616, and may have be
published in that year, though the title page (reproduced on page 1)
dated 1617. The tract was printed by Nicholas Oakes for the booksel
Thomas Archer, who had published Swetnam's *Araignment* two ye
earlier. Appended to the title treatise is a shorter tract, *Certaine Quae
to the bayter of Women*, with a separate title page (reproduced
page 29); it is paginated continuously with the *Mouzell* in all copies,
apparently it was not printed separately. These tracts were printed wi
some care. Decorative elements include a title-page ornament to *C
taine Quaeres*, eleven decorative headings and end pieces, and six elab
rate initial letters. Apparently there was only one impression: none
the eight errors listed as errata are corrected in any of the extant copi
nor are there other variations among the copies. An upside-down hea
ing on page 29 in the Newberry copy indicates that there were at le
two states.

The revised edition of the Pollard and Redgrave *Short-Title Catalog
of Books Printed in English to 1640* (1976–91) identifies eight copi
(STC 23058). Two are at the Houghton Library, Harvard; one is a pe
fect copy and the other is of *Certaine Quaeres* only, with a tipped-in ti
page for that tract. The Huntington copy has only the *Mouzell*, a
lacks *Certaine Quaeres*. The second Houghton copy and the Huntin
ton copy may be two parts of an original complete volume, or may in

te that the two tracts were sometimes bound separately. There are
rfect copies at the British Library (bound with Sowernam's tract and
ur others unrelated to the controversy), and at the Bodleian Library,
e Folger Shakespeare Library, the Newberry Library, and the Beinecke
brary, Yale. The Beinecke copy (Ih Sp 33 617m) is of particular inter-
t for some eighty-five marginal annotations in a contemporary hand,
:fending Swetnam and excoriating Speght. They are discussed and
produced in the appendix. An *ex libris* bookplate on one of the fly-
aves indicates that this copy belonged at some later date to Robert,
arl of Crewe.

Mortalities Memorandum with a Dreame Prefixed was entered into the
ationers' Register on 18 January 1621. It was printed by Edward Grif-
ı for another bookseller, Jacob Bloome, and dated 1621 on the title
ıge (reproduced on page 43). The quarto volume is nicely printed,
ith title page ornament, one ornamental initial letter, three decorative
:adings, and a decorated motto as an endpiece to each of the two
ɔems. There was apparently only one impression: the three errors
ɔted in the errata list are not corrected in any of the extant copies, and
ıere are no other variations among the copies.

The *Short Title Catalogue* identifies six copies (STC 23057) and one
agment, but does not count one of the two copies at the British
ıbrary. One of the British Library copies is in the Greville Collection,
ı fine condition; the other has its pages cropped to fit a smaller bind-
ıg. There is an unmarked copy in the Beinecke Library (Yale) and
ıother at the Huntington Library; the Newberry Library copy has a
ᴠw doodles. The copy at the Houghton Library (Harvard) has crossref-
·ences on pages 9 and 31 to Speght's use of the term "Pretertense," and
ᴠo bookplates identify former owners of this copy as Francis Freeling
ıd Thomas Gaisford. The Folger copy bears the *ex libris* of Sir R.
eicester Harmsworth, Bart, and the seal "Ex Museo Huthii/Animus
on res" [From the Huth Library. The Spirit not the material object].
'here is a fragment at Merton College, Oxford, in the binding of
›aniel Chamierus, *Panstratiae Catholicae...corpus*, vols. 1 and 2
ʒeneva, 1626); it comprises two cropped signatures: the title page,
ɔistle dedicatory, and page 2 of *A Dreame*, and pages 7–10.

The base text for the *Mouzell* and *Certaine Quaeres* is the Hought(Library copy (14462.13.6*). The base text for *Mortalities Memorandu* is the Huntington Library copy (HN 69555). Both are clean, compl(copies, and are used by permission.

Note on the Text

This text reproduces the original spelling and punctuation of both v(umes with the following exceptions: *i, j, u, v,* and *w* have been regula ized to conform to modern usage, and I have silently emended obvio(typographical errors, such as turned letters. Abbreviations have be(silently expanded in the text proper, with the exception of a printed si(nature on page 6 and common Latin forms such as "etc." and "viz, which have been retained. I have also silently corrected the errors not(in the errata lists of both texts (see pages 6 and 90). Where the origin forms may represent what Speght first wrote, I note and discuss them footnotes. One printer's correction in the *Mouzell,* "*Hevahs*" for "*Hero(* (page 16, l. 110), was placed at the end of the text, evidently a late di covery. I have added it to the general errata list, page 6.

I have also corrected a few obvious errors and changed certain co(fusing obsolete forms, as noted below:

Mouzell
"a" for "as" (page 7, l. 13)
"its" for "it" (page 13, l. 49)
"each" for "ech" (page 20, l. 225)
"Antoninus" for "Antonius" (page 22, l. 270)
"Sarcasmus" for "Scarcasmus" (page 35, l. 35)
"you" for "your" (page 37, l. 90, second use)

Mortalities Memorandum
"of" for "off" (pages 45, l. 8, and 78, l. 469)
"off" for "of" (page 45, l. 17)
"*Phoebe*" for "*Phoebus*" (page 48, l. 3)
"shuttle" for "shittle" (page 78, l. 468)
"its" for "it" (pages 79, l. 494, and 86, l. 686).

Speght's *Mouzell* has many biblical citations printed in the margins.
hey are included here among the annotations, set off by the designa-
on "margin," with an indication of the line to which each belongs.
bbreviations (biblical references and forms such as "Object." for
Objection") have been retained in the marginalia to both of Speght's
lumes and in the anonymous handwritten comments on Speght's
ouzell recorded in the appendix.

   In my annotations to Speght's texts, classical works are cited from the
eb Classics by book, chapter, and section numbers, or act, scene, and
e numbers for drama and line numbers for poetry; biblical citations
e to the Authorized (King James) version (1611), in a modern-spell-
g edition.

Selected Bibliography

ilin, Elaine V. *Redeeming Eve: Women Writers of the English Renaissance.*
Princeton: Princeton University Press, 1987, 247–66.

——. "Writing Public Poetry: Humanism and the Woman Writer." *Modern
Language Quarterly* 51 (1990): 249–71.

andall, Coryl. "The Cultural Implications of the Swetnam Anti-Feminist
Controversy." *Journal of Popular Culture* 2 (1968): 136–48.

——. *Swetnam the Woman-hater: The Controversy and the Play. A Critical
Edition with Introduction and Notes.* Lafayette, Ind.: Purdue University Press,
1969.

eertum, Cis van. "A Hostile Annotation of Rachel Speght's *A Mouzell for
Melastomus* (1617)." *English Studies* 6 (1987): 490–96.

enderson, Katherine Usher, and Barbara F. McManus, eds. *Half Humankind:
Contexts and Texts of the Controversy about Women in England, 1540–1640.*
Urbana and Chicago: University of Illinois Press, 1985.

ull, Suzanne W. *Chaste, Silent and Obedient: English Books for Women, 1475–
1640.* San Marino: Huntington Library, 1982, 106–126.

elly-Gadol, Joan. "Early Feminist Theory and the *Querelle des Femmes*, 1400–
1789." *Signs* 8 (Autumn, 1982): 2–28; rpt. in *Women, History, and Theory:
The Essays of Joan Kelly.* Chicago: University of Chicago Press, 1984, 65–
109.

nes, Ann Rosalind. "Counter-attacks on 'the Bayter of Women': Three
Pamphleteers of the Early Seventeenth Century," in *The Renaissance
Englishwoman in Print: Counterbalancing the Canon,* ed. Anne M. Haselkorn
and Betty S. Travitsky. Amherst: University of Massachusetts Press, 1990,
45–62.

Jordan, Constance. *Renaissance Feminism: Literary Texts and Political Mod* Ithaca: Cornell University Press, 1990, 286–307.

Kusanoki, Akiko. "'Their Testament at Their Apron-Strings': The Representati of Puritan Women in Early Seventeenth-Century England," in *Gloria Face: Women, Public and Private, in the English Renaissance,* ed. S. Cerasano and Marion Wynne-Davies. Detroit: Wayne State University Pr 1992, 185–204.

Lewalski, Barbara Kiefer. "Defending Women's Essential Equality: Rac Speght's Polemics and Poems," in *Writing Women in Jacobean Engla* Cambridge, Mass.: Harvard University Press, 1993, 153–75.

Purkiss, Diane. "Material Girls: The Seventeenth-Century Woman Debate," *Women, Texts, and Histories 1575–1760,* ed. Clare Brant and Diane Purk London and New York: Routledge, 1992, 69–101.

Shepherd, Simon, ed. *The Woman's Sharp Revenge: Five Women's Pamphlets fr the Renaissance.* London: Fourth Estate, 1985.

Travitsky, Betty. "The Lady Doth Protest: Protest in the Popular Writings Renaissance Englishwomen." *English Literary Renaissance* 14 (1984): 25 83.

Woodbridge, Linda. *Women and the English Renaissance: Literature and Nature of Womankind, 1540–1620.* Urbana and Chicago: University Illinois Press, 1984, 74–113.

A
MOVZELL FOR
MELASTOMVS,
The Cynicall Bayter of, and foule
mouthed Barker against
EVAHS SEX.

Or an Apologeticall Answere to
that Irreligious and Illiterate
Pamphlet made by *Io. Sw.* and by him
Intituled, *The Arraignement*
of Women.

By Rachel Speght.

PROVERBS 26. 5.
*Answer a foole according to his foolishnesse, lest he bee wise in
his owne conceit.*

LONDON,
Printed by *Nicholas Okes* for *Thomas Archer,* and
are to be sold at his shop in Popes-
head-Pallace. 1617.

---

tle. **A Mouzell for Melastomus:** a muzzle for the black mouth. This page is an
proximation of the title page from the 1617 edition.

tle. **Cynicall:** a play on the Latin *cynicus*, canine, doglike.

tle. **Evahs:** Eve's. Sometimes spelled "Hevahs." See Speght's account of the usual etymology,
ge 15.

To all vertuous Ladies Honou*rable or Worshipfull, and
to all other of* Hevahs *sex fearing God, and loving their
just reputation, grace and peace through
Christ, to eternall glory.*

was the similie of that wise and learned *Lactantius,* that if fire, though
t with a small sparke kindled, bee not at the first quenched, it may
rke great mischiefe and dammage: So likewise may the scandals and
famations of the malevolent in time prove pernitious, if they bee not
ot in the head at their first appearance. The consideration of this
ght Honourable and Worshipfull Ladies) hath incited me (though
ng, and the unworthiest of thousands) to encounter with a furious
emy to our sexe, least if his unjust imputations should continue with-
t answere, he might insult and account himselfe a victor; and by such
conceit deale, as Historiographers report the viper to doe, who in the   10
inter time doth vomit forth her poyson, and in the spring time suck-
the same up againe, which becommeth twise as deadly as the
rmer: And this our pestiferous enemy, by thinking to provide a more
adly poyson for women, then already he hath foamed forth, may
aporate, by an addition unto his former illeterate Pamphlet (intituled
e *Arraignement of Women)* a more contagious obtrectation then he
th already done, and indeed hath threatned to doe. Secondly, if it
ould have had free passage without any answere at all (seeing that *Tac-*
is, *quasi consentire*) the vulgar ignorant might have beleeved his Dia-
licall infamies to be infallible truths, not to bee infringed; whereas   20

dress. **Honourable or Worshipfull:** Aristocratic women are addressed as "Honorable," and
ves of city officials (the mayor, aldermen, presidents of guilds) are addressed as "Worshipful."

e 1. **Lactantius:** Latin church father (c. A.D. 260–340), author of *Institutiorum Libri*
tem, and known as the Christian Cicero for the beauty of his style. Speght almost certainly
d this simile from a collection of commonplaces. The observation about fire can be traced
Quintus Curtius, *De Rebus Gestis Alexandri Magni* 6.3.11.

es 10–13. **Historiographers...former:** a commonplace of nature lore, in, e. g., Edward
psell, *The Historie of Serpents* (London, 1608), 52, 293.

e 15. **evaporate:** give vent to.

e 16. **obtrectation:** detraction, slander, calumny (from Latin, *obtrectare, OED*).

es 18–19. **Tacere...consentire:** Silence implies consent, a proverb drawn from English
mmon law.

now they may plainely perceive them to bee but the scumme of H
thenish braines, or a building raised without a foundation (at least fr
sacred Scripture) which the winde of Gods truth must needs cast dov
to the ground. A third reason why I have adventured to fling this st
at vaunting *Goliah* is, to comfort the mindes of all *Hevahs* sex, both
and poore, learned and unlearned, with this Antidote, that if the fe
of God reside in their hearts, maugre all adversaries, they are hig
esteemed and accounted of in the eies of their gracious Redeemer,
that they need not feare the darts of envy or obtrectators: For shame a
30   disgrace (saith *Aristotle*) is the end of them that shoote such poyson
shafts. Worthy therefore of imitation is that example of *Seneca*, w
when he was told that a certaine man did exclaime and raile agai
him, made this milde answere; Some dogs barke more upon custo
then curstnesse; and some speake evill of others, not that the defam
deserve it, but because through custome and corruption of their hea
they cannot speake well of any. This I alleage as a paradigmatical p
terne for all women, noble and ignoble to follow, that they be
enflamed with choler against this our enraged adversarie, but patien
consider of him according to the portraiture which he hath drawne
40   himselfe, his Writings being the very embleme of a monster.

This my briefe Apologie (Right Honourable and Worshipfull) di
enterprise, not as thinking my selfe more fit then others to underta
such a taske, but as one, who not perceiving any of our Sex to enter t
Lists of encountring with this our grand enemy among men, I being c
of all feare, because armed with the truth, which though often blam
yet can never be shamed, and the Word of Gods Spirit, together wi
the example of vertues Pupils for a Buckler, did no whit dread
combate with our said malevolent adversarie. And if in so doing I sh

---

Line 27. **maugre:** despite.

Lines 29–31. **shame...shafts:** probably from a collection of commonplaces, loosely based
Nicomachean Ethics 4.9.6.

Lines 31–36. **example of Seneca...any:** another commonplace, perhaps a paraphrase fr
Seneca's *De Ira.*

Line 44. **Lists:** area for tilting.

Line 47. **Buckler:** shield.

e censured by the judicious to have the victorie, and shall have given
ntent unto the wronged, I have both hit the marke whereat I aymed,   50
d obtained that prize which I desired. But if *Zoilus* shall adjudge me
esumptuous in Dedicating this my *Chirograph* unto personages of so
gh ranke; both because of my insufficiency in literature and tender-
esse in yeares: I thus Apologize for my selfe; that seeing the *Bayter of
omen* hath opened his mouth against noble as well as ignoble, against
e rich as well as the poore; therefore meete it is that they should be
ynt spectators of this encounter: And withall in regard of my imper-
ction both in learning and age, I need so much the more to impetrate
tronage from some of power to sheild mee from the biting wrongs of
omus, who oftentimes setteth a rankling tooth into the sides of truth.   60
herefore I being of *Decius* his mind, who deemed himselfe safe under
e shield of *Cæsar*, have presumed to shelter my selfe under the wings
 you (Honourable personages) against the persecuting heate of this
erie and furious Dragon; desiring that you would be pleased, not to
oke so much *ad opus*, as *ad animum*: And so not doubting of the
vourable acceptance and censure of all vertuously affected, I rest

> *Your Honours and Worships
> Humbly at commandement.*
>
> Rachel Speght.

---

ne 49. **censured:** judged.

ne 51. **Zoilus:** Greek grammarian and teacher of rhetoric (c. 400–320 B.C.) known for his
acks on Isocrates, Plato, and especially Homer, earning him the title "Homeromastix"
ourge of Homer). The name "Zoilus" came to signify any spiteful and malignant critic.

ne 52. **Chirograph:** a formally written and signed document (originally handwritten).

ne 58. **impetrate:** entreat, request, beseech (from Latin *impetrare*, OED).

ne 60. **Momus:** in Greek myth the son of Night whose frequent lampoons of the gods made
m the personification of censoriousness.

ne 61. **Decius:** This may be the otherwise unknown Decius referred to by Tacitus in "A
ialogue of Oratory" (21): "You won't tell me that anybody reads Caesar's oration in defence
Decius the Samnite." Or possibly P. Decius, a partisan of Antony, who was taken prisoner by
ctavian (later Caesar Augustus) but allowed by him to return safely to Antony (Appian, *Civil
ars*, 4.27). The sentiment is a commonplace: W. Cunningham in dedicating *The
osmographical Glass* (1559) to Robert Dudley, later Earl of Leicester, asks that it "be defended
Tucer was under the shield of mighty Ajax."

nes 64–65. **not...ad animum:** not to look so much to the work as to the intention.

I f Reason had but curb'd thy witlesse will,
O r feare of God restrain'd thy raving quill,
S uch venime fowle thou would'st have blusht to spue,
E xcept that Grace have bidden thee adue:
P rowesse disdaines to wrastle with the weake,
H eathenish affected, care not what they speake.

S educer of the vulgar sort of men,
W as Sathan crept into thy filthie Pen,
E nflaming thee with such infernall smoake,
T hat (if thou had'st thy will) should women choake?
N efarious fiends thy sence heerein deluded,
A nd from thee all humanitie excluded.
M onster of men, worthie no other name,
      For that thou did'st assay our Sex to shame.

RA. S

Faults escaped in this Impression.

Page 7. line 6. in the Preface for *roaring* reade *roaving*.
Page 14. line 57. for *Ironica* reade *Ironia*.
Page 16. line 118. for *not touch* reade *not to touch*.
Page 19. line 203. for *Meriam* reade *Miriam*.
Page 26. line 383. for *tongs* reade *tongues*.
Page 36. line 67. for *adulterous* reade *idolatrous*.
Page 37. line 88. for *Arganox* reade *Organon*.
Page 16. line 110. for *Herods* reade *Hevahs*.

Errata. This list includes printing errors for both *A Mouzell* and *Certain Quaeres*. The page a
line numbers have been changed to the numbers appropriate for the present edition. The fau
noted here have been corrected in the texts.

Not unto the veriest Ideot that *ever set Pen to Paper, but
to the* Cynicall Bayter of Women, or *metamorphosed
Misogunes*, Joseph Swetnam.

ɔm standing water, which soon putrifies, can no good fish be
ɔected; for it produceth no other creatures but those that are ven-
ious or noisome, as snakes, adders, and such like. Semblably, no bet-
ᵗ streame can we looke, should issue from your idle corrupt braine,
ɛn that whereto the ruffe of your fury (to use your owne words) hath
ɔved you to open the sluce. In which excrement of your roaving cogi-
ᴛions you have used such irregularities touching concordance, and
served so disordered a methode, as I doubt not to tel you, that a very
:cidence Schollar would have quite put you downe in both. You
peare heerein not unlike that Painter, who seriously indevouring to   10
urtray *Cupids* Bowe, forgot the String: for you beeing greedie to
ᵗtch up your mingle mangle invective against Women, have not
ɛrein observed, in many places, so much as a Grammer sense. But the
ᵽtiest Barrell makes the lowdest sound; and so we wil accoūnt of
u.

Many propositions have you framed, which (as you thinke) make
uch against Women, but if one would make a Logicall assumption,
ᵉ conclusion would be flat against your owne Sex. Your dealing wants
much discretion, that I doubt whether to bestow so good a name as
ᵉ Dunce upon you: but Minority bids me keepe within my bounds;   20
d therefore I onlie say unto you, that your corrupt Heart and railing
ɔngue, hath made you a fit scribe for the Divell.

In that you have termed your virulent foame, *the Beare-bayting of
ɔmen*, you have plainely displayed your owne disposition to be

---

dress. **Misogunes:** Greek, hater of women (cf. misogynist).

ᴜes 1–3. **From standing water...adders:** a commonplace, see, e.g., Topsell, *Serpents,* 243.

ᴜe 5. **ruffe...words:** Swetnam, *Araignment of Women,* sig. A2: "I being in a great choller
ᴀinst some women, I mean more then one; And so in the ruffe [rough] of my fury, taking my
n in hand...."

ᴜe 9. **Accidence Schollar:** a schoolboy learning his Latin grammar.

ᴜes 10–11. **Painter... String:** This probably refers to a commonplace about omitting what
:rucially important rather than to an actual painting or image.

Cynicall, in that there appeares no other Dogge or Bull, to bayte the
but your selfe. Good had it beene for you to have put on that Muzz
which Saint *James* would have all Christians to weare; *Speake not e*
one of another: and then had you not seemed so like the Serpent *Porp*
rus, as now you doe; which, though full of deadly poyson, yet be
30   toothlesse, hurteth none so much as himselfe. For you having go
beyond the limits not of *Humanitie* alone, but of Christianitie, h.
done greater harme unto your owne soule, then unto women, as m
plainely appeare. First, in dishonoring of God by palpable blaspher
wresting and perverting everie place of Scripture, that you h;
alleadged; which by the testimony of Saint *Peter,* is to the destruction
them that so doe. Secondly, it appeares by your disparaging of, a
opprobrious speeches against that excellent worke of Gods han
which in his great love he perfected for the comfort of man. Third
and lastly, by this your hodge-podge of heathenish Sentences, Simili
40   and Examples, you have set forth your selfe in your right colours, un
the view of the world: and I doubt not but the Judicious will account
you according to your demerit: As for the Vulgar sort, which have
more learning then you have shewed in your Booke, it is likely they w
applaud you for your paines.

As for your *Bugge-beare* or advice unto Women, that whatsoever th
doe thinke of your Worke, they should conceale it, lest in finding fau
they bewray their galled backes to the world; in which you allude to th
Proverbe, *Rubbe a galled horse, and he will kicke:* Unto it I answere
way of Apologie, that though everie galled horse, being touched, do
50   kicke; yet every one that kickes, is not galled: so that you might as w
have said, that because burnt folks dread the fire, therfore none feare f
but those that are burnt, as made that illiterate conclusion which y
have absurdly inferred.

Line 28. margin: James 4.11.

Lines 28–30. **Serpent Porphirus...himselfe:** This toothless but venomous serpent is discus
in Topsell, *Serpents,* 214, though not the quality of hurting only himself.

Line 35. margin: 1.Pet.3.16.

Line 47. **bewray...backes:** reveal (betray) their sensitivity and hence the truth of Swetna
charges, as a horse will kick if touched where it has saddle or harness sores.

In your Title Leafe, you arraigne none but lewd, idle, froward and
inconstant women, but in the Sequele (through defect of memorie as it
emeth) forgetting that you had made a distinction of good from
badde, condemning all in generall, you advise men to beware of, and
not to match with any of these sixe sorts of women, *viz. Good* and
badde, Faire and *Foule, Rich* and *Poore:* But this doctrine of Divells
Saint *Paul* foreseeing would be broached in the latter times, gives warning of.

There also you promise a Commendation of wise, vertuous, and
onest women, when as in the subsequent, the worst words, and filthi-
est Epithites that you can devise, you bestow on them in generall,
excepting no sort of Women. Heerein may you be likened unto a man,
which upon the doore of a scurvie house sets this Superscription, *Heere
is a very faire house to be let:* whereas the doore being opened, it is no
better then a dogge-hole and darke dungeon.

Further, if your owne words be true, that you wrote with your hand,
but not with your heart, then are you an hypocrite in Print: but it is
rather to be thought that your Pen was the bewrayer of the abundance
of your minde, and that this was but a little morter to dawbe up agayne
the wall, which you intended to breake downe.

The revenge of your rayling Worke wee leave to Him, who hath
appropriated vengeance unto himselfe, whose Pen-man hath included
Raylers in the Catalogue of them, that shall not inherit Gods Kingdome, and your selfe unto the mercie of that just Judge, who is able to
save and to destroy.

Your undeserved friend,
RACHEL SPEGHT.

---

line 54. **froward:** peevish, shrewish.
line 60. margin: 1.Tim.4.3.
lines 75–77. **Pen-man hath included Raylers...Kingdome:** See 1 Cor. 6:9–10, "Neither
fornicators, nor idolaters, nor adulterers, nor effeminate, nor abusers of themselves with
mankind. Nor thieves, nor covetous, nor drunkards, nor revilers, nor extortioners, shall inherit
the kingdom of God."

In praise of the Author and her Worke.

If little David *that for* Israels *sake,*
　　esteemed neyther life nor limbe too deare,
In that he did adventure without dread,
　　to cast at him, whom all the hoste did feare,
A stone, which brought Goliah *to the ground,*
Obtain'd applause with Songs and Timbrels sound.

Then let another young encombatant
　　receive applause, and thankes, as well as hee:
For with an enemie to Women kinde,
　　she hath encountred, as each wight may see:
And with the fruit of her industrious toyle,
To this Goliah *she hath given the foyle.*

Admire her much I may, both for her age,
　　and this her Mouzell for a blacke-mouth'd wight,
But praise her, and her worke, to that desert,
　　which unto them belongs of equall right
I cannot; onely this I say, and end,
Shee is unto her Sex a faithfull friend.

PHILALETHE

If he that for his Countrie doth expose
　　himselfe unto the furie of his foe,
Doth merite praise and due respect of those,
　　for whom he did that perill undergoe:
Then let the Author of this Mouzell true
Receive the like, of right it is her due.

Lines 1–6. **If little David...Timbrels sound:** See 1 Sam. 17:4–18:7; **Timbrels:** tambourines
Line 10. **wight:** person.
Line 19. **Philalethes:** lover of truth.

For she to shield her Sex from Slaunders Dart,
    and from invective obtrectation,
Hath ventured by force of Learnings Art,
    (in which she hath had education)   *10*
To combate with him, which doth shame his Sex,
By offring feeble women to perplex.

                                          PHILOMATHES.

Praise is a debt, which doth of due belong
To those, that take the path of Vertues trace,
Meating their wayes and workes by Reasons rule,
Having their hearts so lightned with Gods grace,
    That willingly they would not him offend,   *5*
    But holily their lives beginne and end.

Of such a Pupill unto Pietie
As is describ'd, I doe intend to speake,
A Virgin young, and of such tender age,
As for encounter may be deemd too weake,   *10*
    Shee having not as yet seene twenty yeares,
    Though in her carriage older she appeares.

Her wit and learning in this present Worke,
More praise doth merit, then my quill can write:
Her magnanimitie deserves applaud,   *15*
In ventring with a fierie foe to fight:
    And now in fine, what shall I further say?
    But that she beares the triumph quite away.

                                            FAVOUR B.

---

ne 13. **Philomathes:** lover of knowledge.

ne 3. **Meating:** measuring [meeting].

ne 19. **Favour B:** The name suggests one who applauds or supports, from Latin *favor,*
odwill, support, applause.

A Mouzell for *Melastomus* the *Cynicall Bayter of, and foule*-mouthed Barker against EVAHS Sex.

PROVERBS 18. 22.
He that findeth a wife, findeth a good thing, and receiveth favour of the Lord.

If lawfull it bee to compare the *Potter* with his *Clay*, or the *Architect* w the *Edifice;* then may I, in some sort, resemble that love of God towa man, in creating woman, unto the affectionate care of *Abraham* for sonne *Isaac*, who that hee might not take to wife one of the daughters the *Canaanites*, did provide him one of his owne kindred.

Almighty God, who is rich in mercie, having made all things nothing, and created man in his owne image: that is, (as the Apos expounds it) *In wisedome, righteousnesse and true holinesse; making h Lord over all:* to avoide that solitarie condition that hee was then
10 having none to commerce or converse withall but dumbe creatures seemed good unto the Lord, that as of every creature hee had ma male and female, and man onely being alone without mate, so likew to forme an helpe meete for him. *Adam* for this cause being cast int heavy sleepe, God extracting a rib from his side, thereof made, or bu Woman; shewing thereby, that man was as an unperfect building af woman was made; and bringing her unto *Adam,* united and marri them together.

Thus the resplendent love of God toward man appeared, in taki care to provide him an helper before hee saw his owne want, and in p viding him such an helper as should bee meete for him. Soveraign
20 had hee over all creatures, and they were all serviceable unto him; t yet afore woman was formed, there was not a meete helpe found Adam. Mans worthinesse not meriting this great favour at Gods han but his mercie onely moving him thereunto: I may use those wor

---

Line 5. margin: Gen.24.4.
Line 6. margin: Ephe.2.4.
Line 8. margin: Col.3.30 [probably a printer's mistake for Col.3.3].
Line 9. margin: Ephe.4.24.
Line 13. margin: Gen.2.20.
Line 21. margin: Gen.2.20.

hich the *Jewes* uttered when they saw Christ weepe for *Lazarus, Behold
w hee loved him:* Behold, and that with good regard, Gods love; yea
s great love, which from the beginning hee hath borne unto man:
hich, as it appeares in all things; so next, his love in Christ Jesus appar-
tly in this; that for mans sake, that hee might not be an unite, when
other creatures were for procreation duall, hee created woman to bee
solace unto him, to participate of his sorrowes, partake of his plea-   30
res, and as a good yokefellow beare part of his burthen. Of the excel-
ncie of this Structure, I meane of Women, whose foundation and
iginal of creation, was Gods love, do I intend to dilate.

*Of Womans Excellency, with the causes of her creation, and of
the sympathie which ought to be in man and
wife each toward other.*

he worke of Creation being finished, this approbation thereof was
ven by God himselfe, That *All was very good:* If All, then *Woman,* who,
cepting man, is the most excellent creature under the Canopie of
aven. But if it be objected by any.   40

First, that woman, though created good, yet by giving eare to Sathans
mptations, brought death and misery upon all her posterity.

Secondly, That *Adam was not deceived, but that the woman was
ceived, and was in the transgression.*

Thirdly, that Saint *Paul* saith, *It were good for a man not to touch a
oman.*

Fourthly, and lastly, that of *Salomon,* who seemes to speake against all
f our sex; *I have found one man of a thousand, but a woman among them
l have I not found,* whereof in its due place.

---

ne 24.   margin: John 11.36.

ne 31.   margin: 1. Cor.11.9.

ne 38.   margin: Gen.1.31.

ne 41.   margin: 1 *Object.*

ne 43.   margin: 2 *Object.*

ne 44.   margin: 1. Tim.2.14.

ne 45.   margin: 3 *Object.*

ne 46.   margin: 1. Cor.7.1.

ne 47.   margin: 4 *Object.*

ne 48.   margin: Eccles.7.30.

50   To the first of these objections I answere; that Sathan first assailed ⟨t⟩
woman, because where the hedge is lowest, most easie it is to get ov⟨⟩
and she being the weaker vessell was with more facility to be seduc⟨⟩
Like as a Cristall glasse sooner receives a cracke then a strong stone p⟨⟩
Yet we shall finde the offence of *Adam* and *Eve* almost to paralell: For⟨⟩
an ambitious desire of being made like unto God, was the motive wh⟨i⟩
caused her to eate, so likewise was it his; as may plainely appeare by t⟨h⟩
Ironia, Behold, man is become as one of us: Not that hee was so inde⟨e⟩
but heereby his desire to attaine a greater perfection then God had gi⟨v⟩
him, was reproved. Woman sinned, it is true, by her infidelitie in ⟨n⟩
60 beleeving the Word of God, but giving credite to Sathans faire pro⟨m⟩
ises, that *shee should not die;* but so did the man too: And if *Adam* h⟨⟩
not approoved of that deed which *Eve* had done, and beene willing ⟨⟩
treade the steps which she had gone, hee being her Head would ha⟨⟩
reproved her, and have made the commandement a bit to restraine h⟨i⟩
from breaking his Makers Injunction: For if a man burne his hand ⟨⟩
the fire, the bellowes that blowed the fire are not to be blamed, but hi⟨m⟩
selfe rather, for not being carefull to avoyde the danger: Yet if the b⟨e⟩
lowes had not blowed, the fire had not burnt; no more is woman simp⟨⟩
to bee condemned for mans transgression: for by the free will, whi⟨⟩
70 before his fall hee enjoyed, hee might have avoyded, and beene fr⟨⟩
from beeing burnt, or singed with that fire which was kindled ⟨⟩
Sathan, and blowne by *Eve.* It therefore served not his turne a wh⟨⟩
afterwardes to say, *The woman which thou gavest mee, gave mee of the tr⟨⟩*
and I did eate: For a penalty was inflicted upon him, as well as on t⟨⟩
woman, the punishment of her transgression being particular to h⟨⟩
owne sex, and to none but the female kinde: but for the sinne of m⟨a⟩

Line 50. margin: 1 *Object. answered.*

Line 52. **weaker vessell:** phrase from 1 Peter 3:7, used to describe women in count⟨⟩ marriage sermons and tracts, including the official "Homily on Matrimony."

Line 57. **Ironia:** figure of speech termed the "dry mock" by George Puttenham, *The Art⟨e⟩ English Poesie* (London, 1589), 157, since it is used to dissemble "when ye speake in derision⟨⟩ mockerie." It typically exaggerates or minimizes or states something contrary to truth.

Line 57. margin: Gen.3.22.

Line 61. margin: Gen.3.4.

Line 73. margin: Genesis 3.12.

whole earth was cursed. And he being better able, then the woman, have resisted temptation, because the stronger vessell, was first called account, to shew, that to whom much is given, of them much is required; and that he who was the soveraigne of all creatures visible, [80] ould have yeelded greatest obedience to God.

True it is (as is already confessed) that woman first sinned, yet finde e no mention of spirituall nakednesse till man had sinned: then it is d, *Their eyes were opened,* the eies of their mind and conscience; and en perceived they themselves naked, that is, not onely bereft of that egritie, which they originally had, but felt the rebellion and disobedi- ce of their members in the disordered motions of their now corrupt ture, which made them for shame to cover their nakednesse: then d not afore) is it said that they saw it, as if sinne were imperfect, and able to bring a deprivation of a blessing received, or death on all [90] nkind, till man (in whom lay the active power of generation) had nsgressed. The offence therefore of *Adam* and *Eve* is by Saint *Austin* us distinguished, *the man sinned against God and himselfe, the woman ainst God, her selfe, and her husband:* yet in her giving of the fruit to e had she no malicious intent towardes him, but did therein shew a sire to make her husband partaker of that happinesse, which she ought by their eating they should both have enjoyed. This her giving *lam* of that sawce, wherewith Sathan had served her, whose sowre- sse afore he had eaten, she did not perceive, was that, which made her ne to exceed his: wherefore, that she might not of him, who ought [100] honour her, be abhorred, the first promise that was made in Paradise, d makes to woman, that by her Seede should the Serpents head be oken: whereupon *Adam* calles her *Hevah, life,* that as the woman had ene an occasion of his sinne, so should woman bring foorth the

---

e 78. margin: Genesis 3.17.

es 79–80. **to whom…required:** an unnoted paraphrase of Luke 12:48.

e 84. margin: Genesis 3.7.

es 92–94. **Saint Austin…husband:** St. Augustine. The formula became a commonplace, haps derived (very loosely) from some phrases in Augustine's sermon "De Adam et Eva et cta Maria," ed. Cardinal Angelo Mai, *Novae Patrum Bibliothecae* (Rome, 1852), 1:2.

e 100. margin: 1 Pet. 3.7.

e 102. margin: Genesis 3.15.

Saviour from sinne, which was in the fullnesse of time accomplished;
which was manifested, that he is a Saviour of beleeving women, no l‹
then of men, that so the blame of sinne may not be imputed to his c‹
ture, which is good; but to the will by which *Eve* sinned, and yet
Christs assuming the shape of man was it declared, that his mercie ‹
equivalent to both Sexes; so that by *Hevahs* blessed Seed (as Saint *I*
affirmes) it is brought to passe, that *male and female are all one in Ch*
Jesus.

To the second objection I answer, That the Apostle doth not heer‹
exempt man from sinne, but onely giveth to understand, that
woman was the primarie transgressour; and not the man, but that n
was not at all deceived, was farre from his meaning: for he afterw
expresly saith, that as *in Adam all die, so in Christ shall all be made al.*

For the third objection, *It is good for a man not to touch a woman:* ‹
Apostle makes it not a positive prohibition, but speakes it on‹
because of the *Corinths* present necessitie, who were then persecuted
the enemies of the Church, for which cause, and no other, hee saith, ‹
thou loosed from a wife? seeke not a wife: meaning whilst the time of th
perturbations should continue in their heate; *but if thou art bound, se*
not to be loosed: if thou marriest, thou sinnest not, only increasest thy ca
for the married careth for the things of this world, And I wish that you u
without care, that yee might cleave fast unto the Lord without separati
For the time remaineth, that they which have wives be as though they l
none: for the persecuters shall deprive you of them, eyther by imprisc
ment, banishment, or death; so that manifest it is, that the Apostle d‹
not heereby forbid marriage, but onely adviseth the *Corinths* to forbe‹
a while, till God in mercie should curbe the fury of their adversari‹
For (as *Eusebius* writeth) *Paul* was afterward married himselfe, ‹

Line 106. margin: Galat.4.4.

Line 111. margin: Galat.3.28.

Line 113. margin: 2 *Objection answered.*

Line 117. margin: 1. Cor.15.22.

Line 118. margin: 3 *Objection answered.*

Line 120. margin: 1 Cor.7.

Line 132. **Eusebius:** Bishop of Caesarea and historian of the early church (A.D. 260–340) refers to Paul's marriage in *Ecclesiastical History* 3:30.

ich is very probable, being that interrogatively he saith, *Have we not wer to leade about a wife, being a sister, as well as the rest of the Apostles, d as the brethren of the Lord and Cephas?*

The fourth and last objection, is that of *Salomon, I have found one n among a thousand, but a woman among them all have I not found:* answere of which, if we looke into the storie of his life, wee shall de therein a Commentary upon this enigmaticall Sentence included: it is there said, that *Salomon* had seven hundred wives, and three ndred concubines, which number connexed make one thousand. ese women turning his heart away from being perfect with the Lord God, sufficient cause had hee to say, that among the said thousand men found he not one upright. Hee saith not, that among a thound women never any man found one worthy of commendation, but eakes in the first person singularly, *I have not found,* meaning in his ne experience: for this assertion is to be holden a part of the confesn of his former follies, and no otherwise, his repentance being the tended drift of *Ecclesiastes.*

Thus having (by Gods assistance) removed those stones, whereat me have stumbled, others broken their shinnes, I will proceede ward the period of my intended taske, which is, to decipher the excelncy of women: of whose Creation I will, for orders sake observe; First, e efficient cause, which was God; Secondly, the materiall cause, or at whereof shee was made; Thirdly, the formall cause, or fashion, and oportion of her feature; Fourthly and lastly, the finall cause, the end purpose for which she was made. To beginne with the first.

140

150

---

ne 133. margin: 1.Corint.9.5.

ne 135. **Cephas:** another name for the Apostle Peter (John 1:42), from the Aramaic *kepha,* k (Greek, *petros*).

ne 136. margin: 4 *Object answered.*

ne 137. margin: Eccles.7.30.

ne 142. margin: 1 King.11.3.

ne 144. margin: Pagnine. **Pagnine:** pagan. Solomon's household of one thousand believers is thus an unlikely source of good women.

nes 154–57. **the efficient cause...made:** In Aristotle's definition (*Physics* 2.3, 194b16– 5b30) the efficient cause is the agent by whom or by which something is made. The material se is the matter of which it is made. The formal cause is the pattern or form of the thing de. The final cause is the end or purpose for which it is made.

The efficient cause of womans creation, was *Jehovah* the *Eternall;*
truth of which is manifest in *Moses* his narration of the sixe da
160   workes, where he saith, *God created them male and female:* And *Da*
exhorting all *the earth to sing unto the Lord;* meaning, by a Metonim
earth, all creatures that live on the earth, of what nation or Sex soev
gives this reason, *For the Lord hath made us.* That worke then can r
chuse but be good, yea very good, which is wrought by so excellen
workeman as the Lord: for he being a glorious Creator, must nee
effect a worthie creature. Bitter water can not proceede from a pleas
sweete fountaine, nor bad worke from that workman which is perfec
good, and in proprietie, none but he.

Secondly, the materiall cause, or matter whereof woman was ma
170   was of a refined mould, if I may so speake: for man was created of t
dust of the earth, but woman was made of a part of man, after that
was a living soule: yet was shee not produced from *Adams* foote, to
his too low inferiour; nor from his head to be his superiour, but fro
his side, neare his heart, to be his equall; that where he is Lord, she m
be Lady: and therefore saith God concerning man and woman joint
Let them rule over the fish of the Sea, and over the foules of the Heaven, a
over every beast that moveth upon the earth: By which words, he mal
their authority equall, and all creatures to be in subjection unto the
both. This being rightly considered, doth teach men to make su
180   account of their wives, as *Adam* did of *Eve, This is bone of my bone, a*
flesh of my flesh: As also, that they neyther doe or wish any more hu
unto them, then unto their owne bodies: for men ought to love th
wives as themselves, because hee that loves his wife, loves himselfe: A

Line 160. margin: Genesis 1.28.

Line 161. **Metonimie:** metonymy, a figure of speech in which a part or attribute of a thin;
taken for the whole.

Line 163. margin: Psal.100.3.

Line 167. margin: Psal.100.4 [100.5].

Line 168. margin: Math.19.17.

Line 171. margin: Genesis 2.7.

Line 176. margin: Genesis 1.26.

Line 180. margin: Genesis 2.23.

Line 183. margin: Ephes.5.28.

ver man hated his owne flesh (which the woman is) unlesse a monster
nature.

Thirdly, the formall cause, fashion, and proportion of woman was
ellent: For she was neyther like the beasts of the earth, foules of the
e, fishes of the Sea, or any other inferiour creature, but Man was the
ely object, which she did resemble. For as God gave man a lofty
untenance, that hee might looke up toward Heaven, so did he like-
se give unto woman. And as the temperature of mans body is excel-
t, so is womans. For whereas other Creatures, by reason of their
sse humours, have excrements for their habite, as foules, their feath-
, beasts, their haire, fishes, their scales, man and woman onely, have
eir skinne cleare and smoothe. And (that more is) in the Image of
d were they both created; yea and to be briefe, all the parts of their
dies, both externall and internall, were correspondent and meete each
other.

Fourthly and lastly, the finall cause, or end, for which woman was
ade, was to glorifie God, and to be a collaterall companion for man to
rifie God, in using her bodie, and all the parts, powers, and faculties
ereof, as instruments for his honour: As with her voice to sound
rth his prayses, like *Miriam,* and the rest of her company; with her
ngue not to utter words of strife, but to give good councell unto her
sband, the which hee must not despise. For *Abraham* was bidden to
e eare to *Sarah* his wife. *Pilate* was willed by his wife not to have anie
nd in the condemning of CHRIST; and a sinne it was in him, that hee
ned not to her: *Leah* and *Rachel* councelled *Jaacob* to do according to
e word of the Lord: and the Shunamite put her husband in mind of
rbouring the Prophet *Elisha:* her hands shold be open according to

190

200

210

---

e 191. **temperature:** Many writers, looking back to Aristotle, found a natural basis for
ale inferiority in the preponderance of cold and wet humors in women, by contrast with
hot and dry humors of the male.

e 195. margin: Gen.1.26.

e 203. margin: Exod.15.20.

e 205. margin: Genesis 21.12.

e 207. margin: Math.27.19.

e 208. margin: Genesis 31.16.

e 210. margin: 2 Kings 4.9.

her abilitie, in contributing towards Gods service, and distressed ⟨ser⟩
vants, like to that poore widdow, which cast two mites into the T⟨rea⟩
surie; and as *Marie Magdalen, Susanna,* and *Joanna* the wife of *Her⟨ods⟩*
Steward, with many other, which of their substance ministred u⟨nto⟩
CHRIST. Her heart should be a receptacle for Gods Word, like M⟨arie⟩
that treasured up the sayings of CHRIST in her heart. Her feete sho⟨uld⟩
be swift in going to seeke the Lord in his Sanctuarie, as *Marie Magda⟨len⟩*
made haste to seeke CHRIST at his Sepulchre. Finally, no power exter⟨n⟩
or internall ought woman to keep idle, but to imploy it in some ser⟨vice⟩
220   of GOD, to the glorie of her Creator, and comfort of her owne soule.

   The other end for which woman was made, was to be a Compan⟨ion⟩
and *helper* for man; and if she must be an *helper,* and but an *helper,* then
those husbands to be blamed, which lay the whole burthen of domesti⟨c⟩
affaires and maintenance on the shoulders of their wives. For, as yoa⟨k⟩
fellowes they are to sustayne part of each others cares, griefs, and cala⟨mi⟩
ties: But as if two Oxen be put in one yoke, the one being bigger then ⟨the⟩
other, the greater beares most weight; so the Husband being the stron⟨g⟩
vessell is to beare a greater burthen then his wife; And therefore the L⟨ord⟩
said to *Adam, In the sweate of thy face shalt thou eate thy bread, till th⟨ou⟩*
230   *returne to the dust.* And Saint *Paul* saith, *That he that provideth not for ⟨his⟩*
houshold is worse then an Infidel. Nature hath taught senselesse creatures ⟨to⟩
helpe one another; as the Male Pigeon, when his Hen is weary with sitti⟨ng⟩
on her egges, and comes off from them, supplies her place, that in ⟨her⟩
absence they may receive no harme, untill such time as she is fu⟨lly⟩
refreshed. Of small Birds the Cocke alwaies helpes his Hen to build ⟨her⟩

Lines 212–13. **poore widdow...Treasurie:** In Luke 21:1–4, Christ praises a poor widow's
as surpassing that of rich men, since she gave all she had.   Line 213. margin: Luke 8.

Lines 213–15. **Marie...Christ:** The three women's aid to Christ is noted in Luke 8:1
Susanna later announced the Resurrection; Joanna's husband was healed by Jesus.

Line 216. margin: Luke 1.51.

Line 218. margin: John 20.1.

Line 229. margin: Gen.3.19.

Line 231. margin: 1. Tim.5.8.

Lines 232–35. **as the Male Pigeon...refreshed:** probably from a commonplace collection ⟨and⟩
derived originally from Pliny, *Historia Naturalis* 10.79, "The hen wood-pigeon sits from n⟨oon⟩
till the next morning and the cock the rest of the time....In this species [pigeons] both birds
the cock in the daytime and the hen at night."

st; and while she sits upon her egges, he flies abroad to get meat for her,
ho cannot then provide any for her selfe. The crowing Cockrell helpes
s Hen to defend her Chickens from perill, and will indanger himselfe to
ve her and them from harme. Seeing then that these unreasonable crea-
res, by the instinct of nature, beare such affection each to other, that   240
ithout any grudge, they willingly, according to their kind, helpe one
other, I may reason *à minore ad maius*, that much more should man and
oman, which are reasonable creatures, be helpers each to other in all
ings lawfull, they having the Law of God to guide them, his Word to bee
Lanthorne unto their feete, and a Light unto their pathes, by which they
e excited to a farre more mutuall participation of each others burthen,
en other creatures. So that neither the wife may say to her husband, nor
e husband unto his wife, I have no need of thee, no more then the mem-
rs of the body may so say each to other, betweene whom there is such a
mpathie, that if one member suffer, all suffer with it: Therefore though   250
od bade *Abraham* forsake his Countrey and Kindred, yet he bade him
ot forsake his wife, who being *Flesh of his flesh, and bone of his bone,* was
bee copartner with him of whatsoever did betide him, whether joy or
rrow. Wherefore *Salomon* saith, *Woe to him that is alone;* for when
oughts of discomfort, troubles of this world, and feare of dangers do
ssesse him, he wants a companion to lift him up from the pit of per-
exitie, into which hee is fallen: for a good wife, saith *Plautus*, is the
ealth of the minde, and the welfare of the heart; and therefore a meete
sociate for her husband; And *Woman*, saith *Paul, is the glorie of the man.*

---

nes 235–39. **Of small Birds...harme:** Pliny on house doves is the original source for these
servations (10.52). Philamon Holland's translation, *The Historie of the World. Commonly
lled, The Natural Historie of C. Plinius Secundus* (London, 1601), elaborates the moral:
"hey mate for life. The cock is imperious, though loving...kind they be to them, when they
e about to build, lay, and sit. A man shall see how readie they be, to helpe, to comfort and
inister to them in this case" (290).

ne 242. **à minore ad maius:** from the lesser to the greater.

ne 249. margin: 1. Cor.12.21.

ne 254. margin: Eccles 4.10.

ne 257. margin: Eccles. 4.10.

nes 257–59. **a good wife...husband:** from a commonplace collection, probably paraphras-
g the Roman dramatist Plautus's *Amphitryon* 2.839–42.

ne 259. margin: 1. Cor.11.7.

260   Marriage is a merri-age, and this worlds Paradise, where there
mutuall love. Our blessed Saviour vouchsafed to honour a marri:
with the first miracle that he wrought, unto which miracle matrimon
estate may not unfitly bee resembled: For as Christ turned water i»
wine, a farre more excellent liquor; which, as the Psalmist saith, *Ma*
glad the heart of man; So the single man is by marriage changed from
Batchelour to a Husband, a farre more excellent title: from a solita
life unto a joyfull union and conjunction, with such a creature
God hath made meete for man, for whom none was meete till she v
made. The enjoying of this great blessing made *Pericles* more unwilling
270   part from his wife, then to die for his Countrie; And *Antoninus Pius*
poure forth that patheticall exclamation against death, for deprivi
him of his deerely beloved wife, *O cruell hard-hearted death in bereav*
mee of her whom I esteemed more then my owne life! A vertuous wom·
saith *Salomon, is the Crowne of her husband;* By which metaphor h
sheweth both the excellencie of such a wife, and what account her husba
is to make of her: For a King doth not trample his Crowne under i
feete, but highly esteemes of it, gently handles it, and carefully laies
up, as the evidence of his Kingdome; and therefore when *Dav*
destroyed *Rabbah* hee tooke off the Crowne from their Kings head:
280   husbands should not account their wives as their vassals, but as th·
that are heires together of the grace of life, and with all lenitie and mil
perswasions set their feete in the right way, if they happen to tread aw·

Line 260. **Marriage is a merri-age:** a commonplace in marriage advice books and sermons.

Line 262. margin: John 2.

Line 264. margin: Psal.104.15.

Lines 269–70. **Pericles...Countrie:** Plutarch in his "Life of Pericles" (24) emphasized
great love of that famous Athenian ruler (495–429 B.C.) for Aspasia (a native of Miletus). !
was never his wife (the law forbade his marriage to a foreigner) but he divorced his wife
associate with her until his death. Cf. *The Lives of the Noble Grecians and Romanes Compa*
Together, trans. Thomas North (London, 1579), 181. **Antoninus Pius:** Roman empe·
(A.D. 86–161) known for his integrity, economy, and promulgation of learning and the a·
He honored the memory of his beloved wife Faustina by founding a charity for orphan girls

Line 273. margin: Prov.12.4.

Lines 278–79. **David...Kings head:** It was Joab who destroyed Rabbah; David took the kin
crown for himself.   Line 279. margin: 1. Chron.20.2.

Line 281. margin: 1. Pet.3.7.

ıring with their infirmities, as Elkanah did with his wives barrennesse. The Kingdome of God is compared unto the marriage of a Kings ıne: *John* calleth the conjunction of Christ and his Chosen, a Marge: And not few, but many times, doth our blessed Saviour in the .nticles, set forth his unspeakeable love towards his Church under the e of an Husband rejoycing with his Wife; and often vouchsafeth to l her his Sister and Spouse, by which is shewed that with *God is no ʋect of persons,* Nations, or Sexes: For whosoever, whether it be man or ›man, that doth *beleeve in the Lord Jesus,* such *shall bee saved.* And if ›ds love even from the beginning, had not beene as great toward ›man as to man, then would hee not have preserved from the deluge the old world as many women as men; nor would Christ after his ·surrection have appeared unto a woman first of all other, had it not ene to declare thereby, that the benefites of his death and resurrec- ·n, are as availeable, by beleefe, for women as for men; for hee indif- ·ently died for the one sex as well as the other: Yet a truth ıgainesayable is it, that the *Man is the Womans Head;* by which title yet Supremacie, no authoritie hath hee given him to domineere, or ·sely command and imploy his wife, as a servant; but hereby is he ıght the duties which hee oweth unto her: For as the head of a man is e imaginer and contriver of projects profitable for the safety of his ıole body; so the Husband must protect and defend his Wife from ;uries: For he is her *Head, as Christ is the Head of his Church,* which ·e entirely loveth, and for which hee gave his very life; the deerest ing any man hath in this world; *Greater love then this hath no man,*

290

300

ıe 283. margin: 1. Sam.1.17.

ıe 284. margin: Math.22.

ıe 285. margin: Rev.19.7.

ıe 287. **Canticles:** the Song of Songs, or Canticle of Canticles.

ıe 289. margin: Rom 2.11.

ıe 291. margin: John 3.18.

ıe 299. margin: 1.Cor.11.3.

ıe 305. margin: Ephe.5.23.

ıe 306. margin: Job 2.4.

ıe 307. margin: John 15.13.

when he bestoweth his life for his friend, saith our Saviour: This presid
passeth all other patternes, it requireth great benignity, and enjoyn
310   an extraordinary affection, For *men must love their wives, even as Ch
loved his Church.* Secondly, as the Head doth not jarre or contend w
the members, which *being many,* as the Apostle saith, *yet make but
bodie;* no more must the husband with the wife, but expelling all bit
nesse and cruelty hee must live with her lovingly, and religiou
honouring her as the weaker vessell. Thirdly, and lastly, as hee is
Head, hee must, by instruction, bring her to the knowledge of her C
ator, that so she may be a fit stone for the Lords building. Women
this end must have an especiall care to set their affections upon such
are able to teach them, that as they *grow in yeares, they may grow in gr*
320   *and in the knowledge of Christ Jesus our Lord.*

     Thus if men would remember the duties they are to performe
being heads, some would not stand a tip-toe as they doe, think
themselves Lords and Rulers, and account every omission of perform
whatsoever they command, whether lawfull or not, to be matter of gr
disparagement, and indignity done them; whereas they should consic
that women are enjoyned to submit themselves unto their husbands
otherwaies then as to *the Lord;* so that from hence, for man, ariset
lesson not to bee forgotten, that as the Lord commandeth nothing to
done, but that which is right and good, no more must the husband;
330   if a wife fulfill the evill command of her husband, shee obeies him a
tempter, as *Saphira* did *Ananias.* But least I should seeme too partiall
praysing women so much as I have (though no more then warrant fr
Scripture doth allow) I adde to the premises, that I say not, all wom

---

Line 308. **president:** precedent.
Line 312. margin: 1. Cor.12.20.
Line 314. margin: Col.3.19.
Line 315. margin: 1. Pet.3.7.
Line 317. margin: 1. Cor.14.35.
Line 319. margin: 1. Pet.3.18.
Line 327. margin: Ephes.5.
Line 331. margin: Actes 5.2.

ᵉ vertuous, for then they should be more excellent then men, sith of
Adams sonnes there was *Cain* as well as *Abel,* and of *Noahs, Cham* as
ᵉll as *Sem;* so that of men as of women, there are two sorts, namely,
ᵒod and bad, which in *Mathew* the five and twenty chapter, are com-
ᵉhended under the name of *Sheepe* and *Goats.* And if women were not
ᵃfull, then should they not need a Saviour: but the Virgin *Mary* a pat-
ᵉrne of piety, *rejoyced in God her Saviour: Ergo,* she was a sinner. In the   340
velation the Church is called the Spouse of Christ; and in *Zachariah,*
ᵉkednesse is called a woman, to shew that of women there are both
ᵈdly and ungodly: For Christ would not *Purge his Floore* if there were
ᵒt Chaffe among the Wheate; nor should gold neede to bee fined, if
ᵃnong it there were no drosse. But farre be it from any one, to con-
ᵉmne the righteous with the wicked, or good women with the bad (as
ᵉ Bayter of women doth:) For though there are some scabbed sheepe
ᵃ Flocke, we must not therefore conclude all the rest to bee mangie:
ᵃd though some men, through excesse, abuse Gods creatures, wee
ᵘst not imagine that all men are Gluttons; the which wee may with as   350
ᵒod reason do, as condemne all women in generall, for the offences of
ᵐe particulars. Of the good sort is it that I have in this booke spoken,
ᵃd so would I that all that reade it should so understand me: for if
ᵗherwise I had done, I should have incurred that woe, which by the
ᵖophet *Isaiah* is pronounced against them that *speake well of evill,* and
ᵒuld have *justified the wicked, which thing is abhominable to the Lord.*

ᵐes 335–36. **Adams sonnes...Sem:** Gen. 4:1–14 tells of Cain killing his brother Abel; Gen.
ᵗ1–27 recounts the story of Noah's three sons, in which Ham [Cham] is cursed for looking
ᵃ his father's nakedness, while Shem [Sem] and Japhet were blessed for covering him.

ᵗe 340. margin: Luke 1.47.

ᵗe 341. margin: Zach. 5.7.

ᵗe 343. **Purge his Floore:** "He [Christ]...will thoroughly purge his floor, and will gather the
ᵗeat into his garner, but the chaff he will burn with fire unquenchable" (Luke 3:16–17).

ᵗe 346. margin: Gen.18.25.

ᵗe 355. margin: Esay 5.20.

ᵗe 356. margin: Prov.17.15.

The Epilogue or upshut of the premises.

Great was the unthankefulnesse of *Pharaohs* Butler unto *Joseph*;
though hee had done him a great pleasure, of which the Butler pro
360   ised requitall, yet was hee quite forgotten of him: But farre greater is
ingratitude of those men toward God, that dare presume to speake a
exclaime against *Woman*, whom God did create for mans comf
What greater discredit can redound to a workeman, then to have
man, for whom hee hath made it, say, it is naught? or what greater d
curtesie can be offered to one, that bestoweth a gift, then to have t
receiver give out, that hee cares not for it: For he needes it not? A
what greater ingratitude can bee shewed unto GOD then the opprob
ous speeches and disgracefull invectives, which some diabolicall natu
doe frame against women?
370   Ingratitude is, and alwayes hath beene accounted so odious a vi
that *Cicero* saith, *If one doubt what name to give a wicked man, let h
call him an ungratefull person, and then hee hath said enough.* It was
detested among the *Persians,* as that by a Law they provided, that su
should suffer death as felons, which prooved unthankefull for any g
received. And *Love* (saith the Apostle) *is the fulfilling of the Lawe:* B
where Ingratitude is harbored, there Love is banished. Let men the
fore beware of all unthankefulnesse, but especially of the superlati
ingratitude, that which is towards God, which is no way more palpa
declared, then by the contemning of, and rayling against women, whi
380   sinne, of some men (if to be termed men) no doubt but God will o
day avenge, when they shall plainely perceive, that it had been better
them to have been borne dumbe and lame, then to have used th
tongues and hands, the one in repugning, the other in writing agai
Gods handie worke, their owne flesh, women I meane, whom God ha
made equall with themselves in dignity, both temporally and eterna

---

Line 359. margin: Gen.40.23.

Lines 371–72. **Cicero…enough:** probably from a collection of commonplaces, and lik
based on Cicero's *De Officiis* 2.18.63, "All men detest ingratitude," or *Ad Atticum* 8
"Ingratitude includes all sins."

Line 375. margin: Rom.13.10.

hey continue in the faith: which God for his mercie sake graunt they vayes may, to the glory of their Creator, and comfort of their owne ules, through Christ Amen.

To God onely wise be glorie now and for ever, AMEN.

Certaine
QVAERES
to the bayter of
Women.

WITH

CONFVTATION
of some part of his Dia-
bolicall Disci-
pline.

LONDON,
Printed by *N. O.* for *Thomas Archer,*
and are to be sold at his shop in
Popes-head-Pallace.
1 6 1 7.

This page is an approximation of the title page from the 1617 edition of *Certaine Quæres to the Bayter of Women.* The ornament is not the same as the original.

Title Page. **Quaeres:** queries.

To the Reader.

though (curteous Reader) I am young in yeares, and more defective
knowledge, that little smattering in Learning which I have obtained,
ing only the fruit of such vacant houres, as I could spare from
aires befitting my Sex, yet am I not altogether ignorant of that Anal-
ie which ought to be used in a literate Responsarie: But the Beare-
yting of Women, unto which I have framed my Apologeticall
swere, beeing altogether without methode, irregular, without Gram-
aticall Concordance, and a promiscuous mingle mangle, it would
mit no such order to bee observed in the answering thereof, as a reg-
ar Responsarie requireth.   10
Wherfore (gentle Reader) favorably consider, that as that Painter is
t to be held unskilfull, which having a deformed Object, makes the
e portraiture; no more am I justly to be blamed for my immethodi-
l Apologie, sith any judicious Reader may plainely see, that the Bay-
of Women his pestiferous obtrectation is like a Taylers Cushion, that
botcht together of shreddes, so that, were it not to prevent future
ection with that venome, which he hath, and daily doth sweate out, I
uld have beene loath to have spent time so idlely, as to answere it at
: but a crooked pot-lid well enough fits a wrie-neckt pot, an unfash-
ed shooe a mis-shapen foote, and an illiterate answere an unlearned   20
eligious provocation. His absurdities therein contayned, are so many,
at to answere them severally, were as frivolous a worke, as to make a
appe for a Flea, and as tedious as the pursuite of an Arrow to an
potent man. Yet to prevent his having occasion to say, that I speake of
any, but can instance none, I have thought it meete to present a few of
em to his view, as followeth, that if Follie have taken roote in him, he
ay seeke to extirpate it, and to blush at the sight of that fruit, which he
th already brought foorth; a fruite I call it (not unfitly I hope) because
Crabbe may so be termed, as well as a good Apple. Thus, not

---

e 5. **literate Responsarie:** An educated person would know that a polemic response is
ected to follow the order of the tract being refuted. Rachel here plays on the term for
rgical responses in church.

es 23–24. **pursuite…impotent man:** a man so weak that he cannot retrieve his arrows.

31

30 doubting of the favour of well affected, and of their kinde acceptanc␣
my indevours, of which I desire not applaud, but approbation: I res␣

Your frie␣

RACHEL SPEG␣

The Preface unto the Subsequent.

With edged tooles (saith the old Proverbe) it is ill sporting; but farre n␣
dangerous: yea damnable is it to dally with Scripture, the two-edged Su␣
of the Eternall: *for so to doe is a breach of the third Commandement; ␣*
he that failes in one point, is guiltie of all. If the magnitude of this si␣
had beene considered by the Bayter of Women, the lamentable, yet ␣
reward thereof, as of all other sinnes without repentance, would, if he ␣
but a servile feare, have restrained him from transgressing herein. But as
devoide of all true feare of Gods indignation against wilfull sinners (fo␣
ignorance doth somewhat extenuate a fault, so doth knowledge much ag␣
10 *vate it) he hath made the* exordium *of his brainesicke exhalation aga␣*
women, to be a perverting of a part of holy Writ; ex unguibus leone␣
judge of this Lion by his pawe. For if the fore foot be monstrous, doubt␣
the whole bodie is correspondent thereto. The Porch indeede is fowle, but
that viewes the sequel, as I have done, shall find a laystall of heather␣
Assertions, Similies, and Examples, illiterate composition, irreligious in␣

Line 1. **edged tooles...ill sporting:** The proverb is often rendered, "Meddle not with e␣
tools, Children, Women, and Fools." See Morris P. Tilley, *A Dictionary of Proverbs in␣*
Sixteenth and Seventeenth Centuries (1950), J. 45. The application to Swetnam classes him
fool.

Line 2. **margin:** Hebr.4.12.

Line 3. **third Commandement:** "Thou shalt not take the name of the Lord thy God in v␣
for the Lord will not hold him guiltless that taketh his name in vain" (Exod. 20:7).

Line 4. **margin:** James 2.10.

Line 10. **exordium:** introduction to an oration or formal treatise.

Line 13. **Porch...fowle:** a metaphor (like the lion's paw, above) for the opening of Swetn␣
tract.

Line 14. **laystall:** place where refuse and dung is laid (*OED*).

.

es, and (which is worst) impious blasphemies therein included, filthy rub-
sh, more fitte to be heaped up by a Pagan, then one that beareth the name
a Christian.

   But lest it should not onely be thought, but also said, that I finde fault
here none is; or that I do ill to mislike the Worke, and not make the   20
thor therewith acquainted, that if he please, hee may answer for himselfe:
thinke it not amisse to propose some few Quæres *unto the Bayter of*
omen, which I have abstracted out of his infamous Booke, as himselfe con-
seth it to be in his Epistle to Women.

---

nes 23–24. **as himselfe confesseth it:** Swetnam writes (with tongue-in-cheek), "When my
ry was a little past, I began to consider the blasphemy of this infamous Booke against your
se...my mouth hath uttered that in my fury which my heart never thought" (sig. A3–A7v).

Certaine Quæres to the Bayter
of women, with confutation of
some part of his Diabolicall
Discipline.

If it bee true, asse you affirme, Page 2. line 26. That *women will not g*
thankes for a good turne.

I demand whether *Deborah* and *Hannah* were not women, who bo
of them sang hymnes of thankesgiving unto the Lord; the one for ▌
mercy in granting her victory over *Israels* enemies, the other for ▌
favourable giving unto her a son, which she full oft and earnestly h
desired?

And where-asse you say, Page 4. line 22. *that a woman that hath*
faire face, it is ever matched with a cruel heart, and her heavenly loo
with *hellish thoughts:* You therein shew your selfe a contradictor of Scri
tures presidents: For *Abigail* was a beautifull woman, and tend
hearted; *Rebekah* was both faire of face and pittifull. Many exampl
serving to confute your universall rule might bee produced, but the
are sufficient to dispell this your cloud of untruth. As for your audaci
in judging of womens thoughts, you thereby shew your selfe an usurp
against the King of heaven, the true knowledge of cogitations bei
appropriate unto him alone.

If your assertion, That *a woman is better lost then found, better f*
saken then taken (Page 5. line 4.) be to be credited, me thinkes, gre
pitty it is, that afore you were borne, there was none so wise as to cou
sell your father not to meddle with a woman, that hee might ha
escaped those troubles, which you affirme, that all married men a
cumbred with, Page 2. line 20. As also that hee might not have begott
such a monster in nature *Asse* your selfe, who (like the Priest which f

---

Line 1. **asse:** Here and often after, Speght puns on "as"/"ass."

Line 5. margin: Judg. 5.

Line 6. margin: 1.Sam.1.11.&2.1.

Line 11. margin: 1.Sam.25.3.18.

Line 12. margin: Gen.24.16.18.

Line 16. margin: Math.12.25.

he was Parish Clearke) defame and exclaime against women, as
ough your selfe had never had a mother, or you never beene a child.
You affirme (Page 10. line 18.) that *for the love of women, David pur-*
sed the displeasure of his God: It had beene good that you had cited
e place of story where you finde it, For I never yet in Scripture read,
at the Almighty was displeased with *David* for his love to women, but   30
his lust to *Bathsheba*, which afterward brought forth his adulterous
, and his causing *Uriah* to be murthered.
In saying (Page 10. line. 25.) that *Jobs wife counselled her husband to*
se God, you misconster the Text; for the true construction thereof
ll shew it to bee a *Sarcasmus* or *Ironicall* speech, and not an instigation
blasphemie.
Page 11. line 8. you count it *Wonderfull to see the mad feates of women,*
shee will now bee merry, then sad: but me thinkes it is farre more
nder-foole to have one, that adventures to make his Writing as pub-
ue as an In-keepers Signe, which hangs to the view of all passengers,   40
want Grammaticall Concordance in his said Writing, and joyne
gether *Women* plurall, and *shee* singular, *Asse* you not onely in this
ace, but also in others have done.
Albeit the Scripture verifieth, that God made woman and brought
r to man; and that a prudent wife commeth of the Lord: yet have you
t feared blasphemously to say, *that women sprung from the divell,* Page
. line 26. But being, as it seemes, defective in that whereof you have
uch need (for *mendacem oportet esse memorem*) you suddainely after
, That *women were created by God, and formed by nature, and therefore*

---

es 24–25. **the Priest…Clearke:** The proverb is, "the parish priest forgets that ever he has
n holy water clerk" (i.e., held the lowly office of priest's assistant); it refers to one who denies
origins or his past.

e 32. margin: 2.Sam.11.

e 35. **Sarcasmus:** rhetorical and poetic figure termed by Puttenham the "bitter taunt," to
used "when we deride with a certaine severitie" (*Arte of English Poesie*, 158).

e 39. **wonder-foole:** Here and often after Speght puns on "full"/"fool."

e 44. margin: Gen.2.22.

e 45. margin: Prov.19.14.

e 48. **mendacem…memorem:** "A liar should have a good memory," a proverb, cited in
intilian, 4.2.91.

50 *by policie and wisedome to be avoyded,* Page 16. line 12. An impious c
clusion to inferre, that because God created, therefore to be avoyc
Oh intollerable absurdity!

   *Men I say may live without women, but women cannot live witl
men,* Page 14. line 18. If any Religious Author had thus affirmec
should have wondred, that unto Satans suggestions he had so m
subjected himselfe, as to crosse the Almighties providence and care
mans good, who positively said, *It is not good for man to bee alone;*
being that the sole testimony heereof is your owne *dico,* I marvell
whit at the errour, but heartily wish, that unto all the untruths you h
60 uttered in your infamous booke, you had subscribed your *Dico,* t
none of them might bee adjudged truths: For *mendacis præmium est*
bis eius non adhiberi fidem.

   Page 17. line 5. you affirme, that *Hosea was brought unto Idolatrie*
marrying with a lewd woman, which is as true as the sea burnes; and
proofe thereof you cite *Hosea* 1. in which chapter is no such matter
be found, it onely containing a declaration of the Lords anger agai
the idolatrous Jewes, who had gone a whoring after other Gods,
forth in a parable of an husband and an adulterous wife.

   Page 19. *Theodora a monstrous strumpet, Lavia, Floria, and Lais, u*
70 *three notable Curtizans.*

   Was not that noble Citie of Troy, sacked and spoyled for the faire Hele
Page 21. *Therefore stay not alone in the company of a woman, trusting*

Line 57. margin: Gen.2.18.

Line 58. **dico:** statement [I say or I assert].

Lines 61–62. **mendacis...fidem:** the reward of a liar is to have no credit given to his words

Lines 65–68. **Hosea 1...adulterous wife:** The biblical text bears out Speght's correctio
Swetnam.

Lines 69–70. **Theodora...Curtizans:** Swetnam recounts the stories of these famous class
courtesans in considerable detail, but Speght makes no rejoinder to the specific cases.
might have noted that he mistakes Lavia for Lamia, the Athenian courtesan who seduced k
Demetrius; the stories of Lamia, Lais of Corinth and Flora of Rome are recounted in tale 7
William Painter's *Palace of Pleasure* (1566; rpt. London: Cresset Press, 1929), 3:71–
Swetnam also mistakes Theodora for Theodoté, a famous Athenian courtesan to wk
Socrates and his friends paid a visit (Xenophan, *Memorabilia* 3.11).

owne chastity, except thou bee more strong then* Sampson, *more wise
en Salomon, *or more holy then* David, *for these, and many more have
ene overcome by the sweete intisements of women, Page 22.

I may as well say *Barrabas* was a murtherer, *Joab* killed *Abner* and
nasa, and *Pharaoh Necho* slew *Josiah;* therefore stay not alone in the
mpanie of a man, trusting to thy owne strength, except thou bee
onger then *Josiah,* and more valiant then *Abner* and *Amasa,* for these
d many more have beene murthered by men. The forme of argumen-   80
tion is your owne, the which if you dislike, blame your selfe for pro-
sing such a patterne, and blush at your owne folly, *Quod te posse non
rile credo:* for it is an old saying, how true I know not, that blushing is
igne of grace.

Page 31. line 15. *If God had not made women onely to bee a plague to
an, hee would never have called them necessarie evils.* Albeit I have not
ad *Seaton* or *Ramus,* nor so much as seene (though heard of) *Aristotles
rganon,* yet by that I have seene and reade in compasse of my appre-
nsion, I will adventure to frame an argument or two, to shew what   90
nger, for this your blasphemy you are in.

To fasten a lie upon God is blasphemy: But the *Bayter of women* fas-
ns a lie upon God: *ergo,* the *Bayter* is a blasphemer.

---

ne 76. margin: Luke 23.19, 2.Sam.3.27.

ne 77. margin: 2.Sam.20.10, 2.King 23.29.

nes 82–83. **Quod…credo:** because I cannot easily believe you.

ne 87. **Seaton or Ramus:** John Seton (1498?–1567) wrote what was for nearly a century the
ndard university treatise on logic, the *Dialectica* (London, 1572, and often reissued). Petrus
mus was a French Protestant logician whose system of logic, the *Dialecticae Partitiones*
547), posed a challenge to the logic enshrined in the schools and universities, which was
sed on Aristotle's *Organon* and its codification in scholastic philosophy. Ramist logic was
necially influential in Protestant countries, including England.

nes 87–88. **Aristotles Organon:** Aristotle's *Organon* refers to his six books on logic, central
the Trivium studied in the schools and universities of Europe. The mistake (an initial
ganox that was corrected to *Organon,* see page 6) may be a printer's error but probably
dicates that Speght had not seen that title written.

nes 91–92. **To fasten…blasphemer:** Speght sets forth this and the following proofs as
istotelian syllogisms, with major premise, minor premise, and conclusion.

The Proposition, I trowe, none will gaine-say, the assumption I t
prove,

Whosoever affirmes God to have called women necessary evils, f
tens a lie upon God: For from the beginning of *Genesis* to the end of
Revelation is no such instance to be found: But the *Bayter* affirmes G
so to have called women, *Ergo,* the *Bayter* fastens a lie upon God.

The reward according to Law Divine due
unto the Bayter of women.

Whosoever blasphemeth God, ought by his Law, to die; The *Bay*
of Women hath blasphemed God, *Ergo,* he ought to die the death.
The Proposition is upon record, Leviticus 24. 14. 16. The Assumptio
formerly proved.

If thou marryest a still and a quiet woman, that will seeme to thee t
thou ridest but an ambling horse to hell, but if with one that is froward a
unquiet, then thou wert as good ride a trotting horse to the divell. Page ?
line 13.

If this your affirmation be true, then seemes it, that hell is the peri
of all married mens travailes, and the center of their circumference.
man can but have either a good wife or a bad; and if he have the form
you say he doth but seeme to amble to hell; if the latter, he were as go
trot to the divell: But if married men ride, how travaile Batchelou
surely, by your rule they must go on foote, because they want wiv
which (inclusively) you say are like horses to carry their husbands
hell. Wherefore in my minde, it was not without mature considerati
that you married in time, because it would be too irkesome for you
travaile so tedious a journey on foote.

Now the fire is kindled, let us burne this other faggot. Page 38. line 4
Beware of making too great a fire, lest the surplussage of that fi
effect which you intended for others, singe your selfe.

Line 119. **faggot:** a bundle of sticks (*OED*).

Shee will make thee weare an Oxe feather in thy Cappe. Page 44. line 4.
If Oxen have feathers, their haires more fitly may be so termed then
ir hornes.

Page 50. *line* 28. *There is no joy nor pleasure in this world which may be*
npared to Marriage, for if the husband be poore and in adversitie, then
* *beares but the one halfe of the griefe: and furthermore, his wife will*
nfort him, with all the comfortable meanes she can devise.

Page 51. *line* 16. *Many are the joyes and sweete pleasures in Marriage, as*
our children, etc. 130

Page 34. *line* 5. *There are many troubles comes gallopping at the heeles of*
voman. If thou wert a Servant, or in bondage afore, yet when thou mar-
st, thy toyle is never the nearer ended, but even then, and not before, thou
ingest thy golden life, which thou didst leade before (in respect of the mar-
d) for a droppe of hony, which quickely turnes to be as bitter as worme-
od.

Page 53. *line* 19. *The husband ought (in signe of love) to impart his*
rets and counsell unto his wife, for many have found much comfort and
fite by taking their wives counsell; and if thou impart any ill happe to
* wife, shee lighteneth thy griefe, either by comforting thee lovingly, or else,* 140
bearing a part thereof patiently.

Page 41. *line* 12. *If thou unfouldest any thing of secret to a woman, the*
re thou chargest her to keepe it close, the more shee will seeme, as it were,
th childe, till shee have revealed it.

It was the saying of a judicious Writer, that whoso makes the fruit of
 cogitations extant to the view of all men, should have his worke to
 as a well tuned Instrument, in all places according and agreeing, the
ich I am sure yours doth not: For how reconcile you those dissonant
ices above cited? or how make you a consonant diapason of those dis-
rds wanting harmony? 150

---

es 122–24. **Oxe feather…hornes:** the horn of stag or ox is a sign of cuckoldry, and the
is for endless puns and jibes in the period.

es 145–47. **saying…agreeing:** perhaps a paraphrase of Horace, *Ars Poetica*, ll. 38–45, 372–
3, emphasizing consistency, harmony, and order.

e 149. **diapason:** concord through all the notes of the scale (*OED*).

Page 34. line 19. You counsell all men, to *shunne idlenesse,* and
the first words of your Epistle to Women are these, *musing with my s*
being idle: Heerein you appeare, not unlike unto a Fencer, which tea
eth another how to defend himselfe from enemies blowes, and suff
himselfe to be stricken without resistance: for you warne others,
eschew that dangerous vice, wherewith (by your owne confession) ye
selfe is stained.

    Page 57. line 5. If thou like not my reasons to expell love, then thou m
est trie Ovids *Art, for he counsells those that feele this horrible heate to cc*
160 *their flames with hearbes which are colde of nature as Rew, etc.*

Albeit you doubt not but by some to be reputed for a good Arch
yet heere you shot wide from the truth, in saying without contradicti
of *Ovids* errour, that Rew is of a cold nature: For most Physitions (if
all) both ancient and moderne, holde it to be hote and drie in the th
degree: and experience will tell the user thereof, that the temperature
hote, not colde. And though the sense of tasting, without further tri
doth repell this errour, I doubt not but in citing this prescription, y
have verified the opinion of that philosopher, which said, That there
some, who thinke they speake wisest, and write most judiciously, wh
170 they understand not themselves.

    But, *ut opus ad finem perducam,* sith I have trode my utmost intenc
steppe, though left one path ungone, I meane the *Beare-bayting of W*
dowes unviewed, in that I am ignorant of their dispositions, accounti
it a follie for me to talke of *Robin-hood,* as many doe, that never shot

---

Lines 153–55. **Fencer…resistance:** The allusion is to Swetnam as master of a fencing scho

Lines 159–60. **Ovids Art…Rew:** Ovid, *Remedia Amoris,* proposes various remedies for
heats of love, including the herb rue (l. 801), but he recommends it for sharpening the eyes
and does not indicate that it is "colde of nature." The error Speght points to is Swetnam's, in
summary of Ovid's remedies (*Araignment,* 57–58).

Lines 163–65. **most Physitions…degree:** The naturalist Pliny in *Historia Naturalis* (20
Section 142) characterizes rue as hot and dry by nature; it thereby stimulates hot and dry (
cold and wet) humors in the body, so would not counter the heats of love.

Lines 168–70. **that philosopher…themselves:** the reference may be to Socrates's fam
dictim, "Know thyself."

Line 171. **ut…perducam:** so I may bring this work to an end.

Lines 172–73. **Beare-bayting of Widdowes:** Swetnam's last chapter.

s Bowe, I leave the speculation (with approbation of their *Beare-yting*) to those that regard neyther affabilitie nor humanitie, and shing unto every such *Misogunes,* a *Tiburne Tiffenie* for curation of his olne necke, which onely through a Cynicall inclination will not dure the yoke of lawfull Matrimony, I bid farewell.

> F ret, fume, or frumpe at me who will, I care not,
> I will thrust forth thy sting to hurt, and spare not:
> N ow that the taske I undertooke is ended,
> I dread not any harme to me intended,
> S ith justly none therein I have offended.

---

es 174–75. **talke of Robin-hood…Bowe:** It is folly to speak of something out of one's perience; a proverb, going back at least to Chaucer.

e 177. **Tiburne Tiffenie:** a Tyburn neckcloth (i.e., a hangman's noose).   Tyburn was a nous place of execution in London, near the present Marble Arch.

MORTALITIES
MEMORANDVM,
WITH
A DREAME PRE-
fixed, imaginarie in manner;
reall in matter.

By Rachel Speght.

Liue to die, for die thou must,
Die to liue, amongst the iust.

LONDON
Printed by Edward Griffin for
Iacob Bloome, and are to be sould at his Shop in
Pauls Church-yard at the signe of the Gray-
hound. 1621.

TO THE WORSHIPFULL AND VERTUOUS
*Gentlewoman, her most respected God-*Mother Mrs
Marie Moundford, wife *unto the worshipfull*
Doctour Moundford Physitian.

nongst diversitie of motives to induce the divulging of that to pub-
ue view, which was devoted to private Contemplation, none is wor-
y to precede desire of common benefit. Corne kept close in a garner
:ds not the hungry; A candle put under a bushell doth not illuminate
house; None but unprofitable servants knit up Gods talent in a Nap-
n. These premises have caused the Printing presse to expresse the sub-
quent *Memorandum of Mortalitie,* by which if oblivious persons shall
e incited to premeditation of, and preparation against their last
ure, when inevitable *Death* seazing on them, shall cease their beeing
on earth, I shall with *Jacob* say, *I have enough:* I levell at no other   10
arke, nor ayme at other end, but to have all sorts to marke and pro-
de for their latter end. I know these populous times affoord plentie of
ward Writers, and criticall Readers; My selfe hath made the number
the one too many by one; and having bin toucht with the censures of
e other, by occasion of my *mouzeling Melastomus,* I am now, as by a
rong motive induced (for my rights sake) to produce and divulge this
f-spring of my indevour, to prove them further futurely who have for-
erly deprived me of my due, imposing my abortive upon the father of
e, but not of it. Their varietie of verdicts have verified the adagie *quot*
mines, tot sententiæ, and made my experience confirme that apo-   20
egme which doth affirme Censure to be inevitable to a publique act.

---

ldress. **Doctour Moundford:** Thomas Moundford, a noted London physician with many
ghly placed court and city patients.
ne 4. margin: Mat.5.15.
ne 5. margin: Mat.25.30.
ne 10. margin: Gen.45.28.
nes 17–19. **to prove them further futurely...of it:** to prove to them further by this new
ature] work that I (and not my father as some formerly claimed) was the author of the
ouzell, termed "my abortive" as a modest admission of its imperfections.
nes 19–20. **quot ...sententiae:** many men, many opinions.
nes 20–21. **apothegme:** a terse, pointed saying.

Unto your worthy selfe doe I dedicate the sequel as a testimonie
my true thankefulnesse for your fruitfull love, ever since my beei
manifested toward me, your actions having beene the Character of y
affection; and that hereby the world may witnesse, that the promise y
made for me, when I could make none for myselfe, my carefull frie
(amongst whom I must repute your ever esteemed selfe) have beene c
cumspect to see performed. I would not have any one falsly to thir
that this *Memorandum* is presented to your person to implie in y
defect of those duties which it requires; but sincerely to denote you a
paradigma to others; for what it shews to be done, shewes but what y
have done; yet ere I leave, give me leave to put you in minde of *Pa*
precept, *be not wearie of well-doing, for in due time you shall reape if*
faint not. Thus presenting unto God my supplication, and unto you
operation, the former to him for your safetie, the latter to you for y
service, I ever remaine

30

Your God-daughter in d
obli

RACHEL SPEGH

<hr>

Lines 25–26. **promise...myselfe:** As godmother, Mary Moundford pronounced the baptis
vows in the infant Rachel's name.

Line 31. **paradigma:** model, pattern, example.

Line 33. margin: Gal.6.9.

Lines 34–35. **my operation:** this book.

To the Reader.

Readers too common, and plentifull be;
For Readers they are that can read a, b, c.
And utter their verdict on what they doe view,
Though none of the Muses *they yet ever knew.*
But helpe of such Readers at no time I crave,   5
Their silence, than censure, I rather would have:
For ignorant Dunces doe soonest deprave.

But, courteous Reader, who ever thou art,
Which these my endevours do'st take in good part,
Correcting with judgement the faults thou do'st finde,   10
With favour approving what pleaseth thy minde.
To thee for thy use, and behoofe, I extend
This poore Memorandum *of our latter end.*
Thus wishing thee wellfare, I rest a true friend.

To those which (Art affect,
And learnings fruit) respect.

RACHEL SPEGHT.

The Dreame.

When splendent *Sol,* which riseth in the East,
Returning thence tooke harbour in the West;
When *Phoebe* layd her head in *Titans* lap,
And Creatures sensitive made hast to rest;
When skie which earst look't like to azure blew,
Left colour bright, and put on sable hew.

Then did *Morpheus* close my drowsie eyes,
And stood as Porter at my sences dore,
Diurnall cares excluding from my minde;
Including rest, (the salve for labours sore.)
Nights greatest part in quiet sleepe I spent,
But nothing in this world is permanent.

For ere *Aurora* spread her glittering beames,
Or did with roabes of light her selfe invest,
My mentall quiet sleepe did interdict,
By entertaining a nocturnall guest.
A *Dreame* which did my minde and sense possesse,
With more then I by Penne can well expresse.

Line 3. **Phoebe...Titans lap:** Speght, or more likely the printer, unaccountably substitu
"Phoebus" for "Phoebe," often identified with Artemis, goddess of the moon.   Here, howe
the reference seems to be to the Titaness Phoebe, whose name means brightness or radia
and whose union with the Titan Coeus resulted in the birth of Leto, mother of Apollo
Artemis (Hesiod, *Theogony,* ll. 136, 404–6). The Titans were ancient gods defeated by Z
and the Olympian dieties, cast out of the heavens, and immured in Tartarus, far beneath
earth. The line seems to refer to Phoebe (brightness) now gone to sleep with her Titan ma
Tartarean darkness.

Line 7. **Morpheus:** Greek god of dreams.

Line 13. **Aurora:** Roman goddess of the dawn.

At the appoyntment of supernall power,
By instrumentall meanes me thought I came   20
Into a place most pleasant to the eye,
Which for the beautie some did *Cosmus* name,
Where stranger-like on every thing I gaz'd,
But wanting wisedome was as one amaz'd.

Upon a sodeyne, as I gazing stood,   25
Thought came to me, and ask't me of my state,
Inquiring what I was, and what I would,
And why I seem'd as one disconsolate:
To whose demand, I thus againe replide,
I, as a stranger in this place abide.   30

The Haven of my voyage is remote,
I have not yet attain'd my journeyes end;
Yet know I not, nor can I give a guesse,
How short a time I in this place shall spend.
For that high power, which sent me to this place,   35
Doth onely know the period of my race.

The reason of my sadnesse at this time,
Is, 'cause I feele my selfe not very well,
Unto you I shall much obliged bee,
If for my griefe a remedie you'le tell.   40
Quoth shee, if you your maladie will show,
My best advise I'le willingly bestow.

My griefe, quoth I, is called *Ignorance,*
Which makes me differ little from a brute:
For animals are led by natures lore,   45
Their seeming science is but customes fruit;
When they are hurt they have a sense of paine;
But want the sense to cure themselves againe.

And ever since this griefe did me oppresse,
Instinct of nature is my chiefest guide;
I feele disease, yet know not what I ayle,
I finde a sore, but can no salve provide;
I hungry am, yet cannot seeke for foode;
Because I know not what is bad or good.

And sometimes when I seeke the golden meane,
My weaknesse makes me faile of mine intent,
That suddenly I fall into extremes,
Nor can I see a mischiefe to prevent;
But feele the paine when I the perill finde,
Because my maladie doth make me blinde.

What is without the compasse of my braine,
My sicknesse makes me say it cannot bee;
What I conceive not, cannot come to passe;
Because for it I can no reason see.
I measure all mens feet by mine owne shooe,
And count all well, which I appoint or doe.

The pestilent effects of my disease
Exceed report, their number is so great;
The evils, which through it I doe incur,
Are more then I am able to repeat.
Wherefore, good *Thought,* I sue to thee againe,
To tell me how my cure I may obtaine.

Quoth she, I wish I could prescribe your helpe;
Your state I pitie much, and doe bewaile;
But for my part, though I am much imploy'd,
Yet in my judgement I doe often faile.
And therefore I'le commend unto your triall
Experience, of whom take no deniall.

For she can best direct you, what is meet
To worke your cure, and satisfie your minde;   80
I thank't her for her love, and tooke my leave,
Demanding where I might *Experience* finde.
She told me if I did abroad enquire,
'Twas likely *Age* could answer my desire.

I sought, I found, She ask't me what I would;   85
Quoth I, your best direction I implore:
For I am troubled with an irkesome griefe,
Which when I nam'd, quoth she declare no more:
For I can tell as much, as you can say,
And for your cure I'le helpe you what I may.   90

The onely medicine for your maladie,
By which, and nothing else your helpe is wrought,
Is *Knowledge,* of the which there is two sorts,
The one is good, the other bad and nought;
The former sort by labour is attain'd,   95
The latter may without much toyle be gain'd.

But 'tis the good, which must effect your cure,
I pray'd her then, that she would further show,
Where I might have it, that I will, quoth shee,
In *Eruditions* garden it doth grow: 100
And in compassion of your woefull case,
Industrie shall conduct you to the place.

Disswasion hearing her assigne my helpe,
(And seeing that consent I did detect)
Did many remoraes to me propose,   105

---

e 105. **remoraes:** hindrances.

As dulnesse, and my memories defect;
The difficultie of attaining lore,
My time, and sex, with many others more.

Which when I heard, my minde was much perplext,
And as a horse new come into the field,
Who with a Harquebuz at first doth start,
So did this shot make me recoyle and yeeld.
But of my feare when some did notice take,
In my behalfe, they this reply did make.

First quoth *Desire, Disswasion,* hold thy peace,
These oppositions come not from above:
Quoth *Truth,* they cannot spring from reasons roote,
And therefore now thou shalt no victor prove.
No, quoth *Industrie,* be assured this,
Her friends shall make thee of thy purpose misse.

For with my sickle I will cut away
All obstacles, that in her way can grow,
And by the issue of her owne attempt,
I'le make thee *labor omnia vincet* know.
Quoth *Truth,* and sith her sex thou do'st object,
Thy folly I by reason will detect.

Line 107. **lore:** knowledge.

Line 111. **Harquebuz:** harquebus, an early type of portable gun, mounted on a tripod
carriage in the field.

Line 124. **labor omnia vincet:** Labor will conquer all, an allusion to Virgil's *Georgics* 1.1
"labor omnia vicit," labor conquered all things. Speght's transformed romance garden
recalls Virgil's *Eclogue* 10.69, "omnia vincit amor," love conquers all, and the ambiguous me
of Chaucer's Prioress, "Amor vincit omnia," *Canterbury Tales,* General Prologue, l. 162.

Both man and woman of three parts consist,
Which *Paul* doth bodie, soule, and spirit call: *1.Thess.*5.23.
And from the soule three faculties arise,
The mind, the will, the power; then wherefore shall   130
A woman have her intellect in vaine,
Or not endevour *Knowledge* to attaine.

The talent, God doth give, must be imploy'd,   *Luke* 19.23.
His owne with vantage he must have againe:
All parts and faculties were made for use;   135   *1.Sam.*2.3.
The God of *Knowledge* nothing gave in vaine.
'Twas *Maries* choyce our Saviour did approve,   *Luke* 10.42.
Because that she the better part did love.

Cleobulina, and *Demophila*,
With *Telesilla*, as Historians tell,   140
(Whose fame doth live, though they have long bin dead)
Did all of them in Poetrie excell.
A Roman matron that *Cornelia* hight,
An eloquent and learned style did write.

---

e 139. **Cleobulina, and Demophila:** Cleobulina (fl. 6th century B.C.) was named Eumetus
 was better known from her father, Cleobulus of Rhodes, one of the
en sages. She was celebrated for her skill in composing riddles in hexameter verse, and by
ales for her "statesman's mind" and eagerness to learn medical arts (Plutarch, *Moralia*
B.D). Damophyle (c. 600 B.C.), lyric poet of Pamphilia, was the author of erotic poems and
nns to Artemis. A pupil and intimate companion of Sappho, she also instructed other
men in poetry (Philostratus, *Vita Apollonius* 1.30).

e 140. **Telesilla:** lyric poet (fl. c. 510 B.C.), one of the so-called nine lyric muses who
nposed odes, hymns to the gods, and also battle songs. A heroine of Athens, she led a band
her countrywomen against the Spartans in the Peloponnesian War (Plutarch, "On the
tue of Women," *Moralia* 245 D, E).

e 141. **dead):** The word is missing in the Huntington Library base text (probably broken
e) and is supplied from a British Library copy.

e 143. **Cornelia:** Daughter of P. Scipio Africanus and mother of the two Gracchi tribunes,
erius and Caius, she was often identified as the source of their virtues and oratory. Her
ters show, says Cicero (*Brutus* 58. 211), that her sons "were nursed not less by their mother's
ech than at her breast." (Cf. Plutarch, "Life of Tiberius Gracchus" 1, "Life of Caius
acchus" 4).

Hypatia in Astronomie had skill,
Aspatia was in Rheth'ricke so expert,
As that Duke *Pericles* of her did learne;
Areta did devote her selfe to art:
And by consent (which shewes she was no foole)
She did succeed her father in his schoole.

And many others here I could produce,
Who were in Science counted excellent;
But these examples which I have rehearst,
To shew thy error are sufficient.
Thus having sayd, she turn'd her speech to mee,
That in my purpose I might constant bee.

My friend, quoth she, regard not vulgar talke;
For dung-hill Cocks at precious stones will spurne,
And swine-like natures prize not cristall streames,
Contemned mire, and mud will serve their turne.

Line 145. **Hypatia:** (c. A.D. 370–415), daughter of Theon of Alexandria, who instructed
in philosophy and mathematics. She presided over the neoplatonic school of Plotinu
Alexandria, and wrote works on astronomy, algebra, conic sections, and other topics. A pa
who refused to convert to Christianity, she met her death at the hands of the Christian cle
who accused her of plotting against them with Orestes, prefect of Alexandria, and tore her l
from limb (Socrates Scholasticus, *Historia Ecclesiastica* 7.15).

Line 146. **Aspatia:** Aspasia (470–410 B.C.), daughter of Axiochus and beloved of Pericles
footnote below). Her house was the center of the best literary and philosophical societ
Athens. In Plato's *Menexenus,* Socrates describes her (perhaps ironically) as his own teache
rhetoric, and delivers a funeral oration that he identifies as her composition; he also says
she taught rhetoric to Pericles and composed his famous funeral oration. After Pericles's d
she attached herself to Lysicles, a cattle-dealer, and made him a first-rate orator (Plutarch, "
of Pericles" 24).

Line 147. **Duke Pericles:** (490–429 B.C.), a powerful orator, commander of the Ather
armies, and for ten years head of the Athenian state. (Speght's honorific, "Duke," plays on
Latin "dux," leader, commander). He was famous for his oration counselling the Athenians
to yield to the demands of Sparta, thereby sparking the Peloponnesian War, and also for
funeral oration honoring the fallen (Thucydides, 2.35–46).

Line 148. **Areta:** Arete (fl. 370–340 B.C.), daughter of Aristippus, founder of the Cyre
school of philosophy. Succeeding him as head of the school, she reportedly taught nat
science, moral philosophy, and ethics in Attica for thirty-five years, and wrote more than f
books (Diogenes Laertes, 2.72, 86).

Good purpose seldome oppositions want:
But constant mindes *Disswasion* cannot daunt.

Shall every blast disturbe the Saylors peace?
Or boughes and bushes Travellers affright?
True valour doth not start at every noyse;   165
Small combates must instruct for greater fight.
Disdaine to bee with every dart dismayd;
'Tis childish to be suddenly affrayd.

If thou didst know the pleasure of the place,
Where *Knowledge* growes, and where thou mayst it gaine;   170
Or rather knew the vertue of the plant,
Thou would'st not grudge at any cost, or paine,
Thou canst bestow, to purchase for thy cure
This plant, by which of helpe thou shalt be sure.

Let not *Disswasion* alter thy intent;   175
'Tis sinne to nippe good motions in the head;
Take courage, and be constant in thy course,
Though irkesome be the path, which thou must tread.
Sicke folkes drinke bitter medicines to be well,
And to injoy the nut men cracke the shell.   180

When *Truth* had ended what shee meant to say,
Desire did move me to obey her will,
Whereto consenting I did soone proceede,
Her counsell, and my purpose to fulfill;
And by the helpe of *Industrie* my friend,   185
I quickly did attaine my journeyes end.

Where being come, *Instructions* pleasant ayre
Refresht my senses, which were almost dead,
And fragrant flowers of sage and fruitfull plants,
Did send sweete savours up into my head;   190

And taste of science appetite did move,
To augment *Theorie* of things above.

There did the harmonie of those sweete birds,
(Which higher soare with Contemplations wings,
Then barely with a superficiall view,
Denote the value of created things.)
Yeeld such delight as made me to implore,
That I might reape this pleasure more and more.

And as I walked wandring with *Desire*,
To gather that, for which I thither came;
(Which by the helpe of *Industrie* I found)
I met my old acquaintance, *Truth* by name;
Whom I requested briefely to declare,
The vertue of that plant I found so rare.

*Col.*3.10.

Quoth shee, by it Gods image man doth beare,
Without it he is but a humane shape,
Worse then the Devill; for he knoweth much;
Without it who can any ill escape?
By vertue of it evils are withstood;

*Prov.*19.2.

The minde without it is not counted good.

Who wanteth *Knowledge* is a Scripture foole,
Against the *Ignorant* the Prophets pray;
And *Hosea* threatens judgement unto those,
Whom want of *Knowledge* made to runne astray.
Without it thou no practique good canst show,
More then by hap, as blind men hit a Crow.

Line 191. **appetite:** longing.
Lines 213–14. **Hosea...astray:** See Hosea 4:1–6.
Line 216. **by hap:** by chance, happenstance.

True *Knowledge* is the Window of the soule,
Through which her objects she doth speculate;
It is the mother of faith, hope, and love;
Without it who can vertue estimate?   220
By it, in grace thou shalt desire to grow;
'Tis life eternall God and Christ to *Know*.   *John* 17.3.

Great *Alexander* made so great account,
Of *Knowledge,* that he oftentimes would say,
That he to *Aristotle* was more bound   225
For *Knowledge,* upon which *Death* could not pray,
Then to his Father *Phillip* for his life,
Which was uncertaine, irkesome, full of strife.

This true report put edge unto *Desire*,
Who did incite me to increase my store,   230
And told me 'twas a lawfull avarice,
To covet *Knowledge* daily more and more.
This counsell I did willingly obey,
Till some occurrence called me away.

And made me rest content with that I had,   235
Which was but little, as effect doth show;
And quenched hope for gaining any more,
For I my time must other-wayes bestow.
I therefore to that place return'd againe,
From whence I came, and where I must remaine.   240

---

ne 218. **speculate:** view.

nes 223–27. **Alexander...life:** Aristotle directed the education of Alexander the Great, son
Philip of Macedon.

ne 234. **some occurrence:** The specific occasion is not clear but it took place, lines 241–46
ggest, just before Speght's answer to Swetnam. That would mean 1616, when Speght was
hteen or nineteen. See introduction, page xvii.

But by the way I saw a full fed Beast,
Which roared like some monster, or a Devill,
And on *Eves* sex he foamed filthie froth,
As if that he had had the falling evill;
To whom I went to free them from mishaps,
And with a *Mouzel* sought to binde his chaps.

But, as it seemes, my moode out-run my might,
Which when a selfe-conceited Creature saw,
Shee past her censure on my weake exployt,
And gave the beast a harder bone to gnaw;
Haman shee hangs, 'tis past he cannot shun it;
For *Ester* in the Pretertense hath done it.

And yet her enterprize had some defect,
The monster surely was not hanged quite:
For as the childe of *Prudence* did conceive,
His throat not stop't he still had power to bite.
She therefore gave to *Cerberus* a soppe,
Which is of force his beastly breath to stoppe.

Line 241. **full fed Beast**: Swetnam.

Line 244. **falling evill**: epilepsy.

Lines 251–52. **Haman…Ester in the Pretertense hath done it**: Ester Sowernam (punning Swe[e]tnam), was the pseudonymous author of *Ester Hath Hang'd Haman* (London, 16?. For the story of the biblical Esther who saved the Jewish people from their enemy Haman . brought about his death, see Esther 3–7. The pretertense is the Latin past tense: Spe comments ironically on Sowernam's title as an indication of her self-importance in claimin; have finished off Swetnam entirely, and thereby to have far surpassed Speght's effort. introduction, page xix.

Lines 255–58. **childe of Prudence…to stoppe**: In her answer to Swetnam, *The Worming mad Dogge: Or, a Soppe for Cerberus the Jaylor of Hell* (London, 1617), the pseudonym author Constantia Munda [Pure Constancy] identifies herself as the daughter of a pseu nymous aristocratic mother, Lady Prudentia Munda [Pure Prudence]. Cerberus, in Greek Roman myth, was the three-headed dog with a thunderously loud bark who guarded passage to and from Hades. Aeneas was able to enter only after the Sibyl threw Cerber drugged morsel, which put him to sleep (*Aeneid* 6.417–25).

But yet if he doe swallow downe that bit,
Shee other-wayes hath bound him to the peace;   260
And like an Artist takes away the cause,
That the effect by consequence may cease.
This franticke dogge, whose rage did women wrong,
Hath Constance worm'd to make him hold his tongue.

Thus leaving them I passed on my way,   265
But ere that I had little further gone,
I saw a fierce insatiable foe,
Depopulating Countries, sparing none;
Without respect of age, sex, or degree,
It did devoure, and could not daunted be.   270

Some fear'd this foe, some lov'd it as a friend;
For though none could the force of it withstand,
Yet some by it were sent to *Tophets* flames,
But others led to heavenly *Canaan* land.
On some it seazed with a gentle power,   275
And others furiously it did devoure.

The name of this impartiall foe was *Death*,
Whose rigour whil'st I furiously did view,
Upon a sodeyne, ere I was aware;
With pearcing dart my mother deare it slew;   280
Which when I saw it made me so to weepe,
That teares and sobs did rouze me from my sleepe.

But, when I wak't, I found my dreame was true;
For *Death* had ta'ne my mothers breath away,
Though of her life it could not her bereave,   285
Sith shee in glorie lives with Christ for aye;

---

273. **Tophets:** Hell's.

Which makes me glad, and thankefull for her blisse,
Though still bewayle her absence, whom I misse.

A sodeine sorrow peirceth to the quicke,
Speedie encounters fortitude doth try;
Unarmed men receive the deepest wound,
Expected perils time doth lenifie;
Her sodeine losse hath cut my feeble heart,
So deepe, that daily I indure the smart.

The roote is kil'd, how can the boughs but fade?
But sith that *Death* this cruell deed hath done,
I'le blaze the nature of this mortall foe,
And shew how it to tyranize begun.
The sequell then with judgement view aright,
The profit may and will the paines requite.

Esto Memor Mortis.

Line 292. **lenifie:** mitigate, soften, assuage (*OED*).
Epigraph. **Esto Memor Mortis:** Thou shalt be mindful of death.

Mortalities Memorandum.

When *Elohim* had given time beginning,
In the beginning God began to make   Gen.1. 1.
The heavens, and earth, with all that they containe,
Which were created for *his Glories sake;*   Prov.16.4.
And to be Lord of part of worke or'e-past,   5
He *Adam* made, and *Eve* of him at last.

In *Eden* garden God did place them both,
To whom Commaund of all the trees he gave,
The fruit of one tree onely to forbeare,
On paine of *Death* (his owne he did but crave,)   10
And Sathan thinking this their good too great,
Suggests the Woman, shee the man, they eate.

Thus eating both, they both did joyntly sinne,
And *Elohim* dishonoured by their act;
Doth ratifie, what he had earst decreed,   15
That *Death* must be the wages of their fact;   Gen.2.17.
 Thus on them, and their of-spring thenceforth seaz'd
Mortalitie, because they God displeas'd.

In *Adam all men die,* not one that's free   1.*Cor.*15.22.
From that condition we from him derive,   20
By sinne *Death* entred, and began to raigne,
But yet in *Christ shall all be made alive.*   Rom.5.12.
Who did triumph o're sinne, o're *Death,* and hell,
That all his chosen may in glorie dwell.

---

ne 1. **Elohim:** Hebrew name for God.

nes 9–10. **The fruit...crave:** God's command not to eat of the Tree of Knowledge of Good
d Evil merely proclaimed God's proper right to Adam and Eve's obedience, which this
ohibition tested. See Gen. 2:16–18.

ne 15. **earst:** erst, earlier (*OED*).

ne 16. **fact:** deed.

61

Considering then *Jehovahs* just decree,
That man shall surely taste of *Death* through sinne,
I much lament, when as I mete in minde,
The dying state securely men live in;
Excluding from their memories that day,
When they from hence by *Death* must passe away.

*Ephes.*2.1.

The Scripture mentioneth three kindes of *Death,*
The first whereof is called *Death* in sinne,
When as the bodie lives, and soule is *Dead,*
This sort of *Death* did other *Deaths* beginne.

1. *Tim.*5.6.

The Widowes, whom Saint *Paul* doth specifie,
Their life in pleasure caus'd their soules to die.

The unregenerated sinnefull man,
That seemes to live, but is in spirit *Dead,*
Lives to the world, and daily dies to *God,*
Prepostrously his course of life is led;
He lives and *dies,* but cannot *die* and live,

*Mat.*15.26.

The Childrens bread to Whelps God will not give.

*Rom.*6.11.

The second kinde of *Death* is *Death to sinne,*
Whereby the faithfull and regenerate man
Doth daily *Mortifie* his ill desires,
That *sin* doth neither raigne in him, nor can.
Thus *dying* in this life, in *Death* he lives,
And after *Death* to him God glorie gives.

The third and last of these, is *Death by sinne,*
Which as a roote two braunches forth doth send,
The former bough whereof is *Corp'rall Death,*
The latter *Death eternall* without end.
Which end without end God doth destinate,
To be the stipend of the Reprobate.

Line 27. **mete:** measure, appraise (*OED*).

This is that *Death* which sacred Scripture calls   55
The second *Death,* or separation
Of soule, and bodie from the love of God;
The sinners lot, just Condemnation.
Which *cannot be to them, that are in Christ,*   *Rom.*8.1.
Whose life is hid with him in God the hyest.   60   *Col.*3.3.

A *Corp'rall Death* is common unto all,
To young, and old, to godly and unjust;
The Prince, that swayes the scepter of a Realme,
Must with his Subjects turne by *Death* to dust.
This is the period of all *Adams* lyne,   65
Which Epilogue of life I thus define.

When soule and bodie by one spirit knit,
Unloosed are, and *dust returnes to earth,*   *Eccle.*12.7.
The spirit unto God that gave it man,
By which he lives in wombe before his birth;   70
The bodie voyd of soule, bereft of breath,
Is that condition called *Corp'rall Death.*

This is that *Death,* which leades the soule to life,
This is that friend, which frees us from our paine,
This is the Portall of true Paradise,   75
Through which we passe eternall life to gaine;
This is the leader unto joy or woe,
This is the dore, through which all men must goe.

Death was at first inflicted as a curse,   *Gen.*3.19.
But *Womans seede hath brooke the Serpents head,*   80   *Gen.*3.15.
His bitter *Death* for us hath gained life,
His agonie hath freed his owne from dread.

---

e 66. **Epilogue:** the concluding section or scene that rounds out or comments on a play or
er literary work.

Death is that guest the godly wish to see;
For when it comes, their troubles ended be.

*Rom.*8.1.

All things doe worke together for the best
To those, that love and are beloved of God;
If all things, then must also sinne and *Death*,
Sicknesse, and sorrowes, worlds owne scourging rod:
For in despight of flesh, the world, and Devill,
God to his Children brings good out of evill.

First, we by *Death* are freed from present woe,
And such Gods spirit hath pronounced blest,
As in the Lord depart this irkesome life;
*Revel.*14.13.   For *from their labours they for ever rest.*
'Tis *Death* Conducts us to the land of peace,
Then welcome *Death,* which doth all sorrowes cease.

If man were fettred in a loathsome goale,
Without one sparke of hope to come from thence,
Till Prison walls were levell with the ground,
He would be glad to see their fall Commence.
Thy bodies ruine then rejoyce to see,
That out of Goale thy soule may loosed be.

What worse Bocardo for the soule of man,
Then is the bodie, which with filth is fraught;
Witnesse the sinkes thereof, through which doe passe
The excrements, appoynted for the draught.
Evacuations, loathsome in their smell,
Egested filth, unfit for tongue to tell.

Line 97. **goale:** gaol, jail.
Line 103. **Bocardo:** a prison or dungeon (*OED*).

From out of Prison bring my soule O Lord,   *Psal.*142.7.
Was *Davids* earnest and sincere desire,   110
Eliah in the anguish of his heart,   1.*King.*19.4.
Did *Death* in stead of irkesome life require.
Vile, Live, and *Evil,* have the selfe same letters,
He *lives* but *vile* whom *evil* houlds in fetters.

The Heathens make report, that *Argia,*   115
To yeeld requitall for the toyle and paine,
Which *Biton* and *Cleobis* for her tooke,
Desir'd the goddesse *Juno,* they might gaine
The greatest good, she could to man bequeath,
Which graunted was, and paid with sodeine *Death.*   120

The *Thracians* sadly sorrow and lament,
When as their Children first behold the light,
But with great exultation they rejoyce,
What time their friends doe bid the world *Good-night.*
When *Davids* Childe was sicke he would not eate,   125   2 *Sam.*12.20.
But being *Dead,* he rose and call'd for meate.

By *Death* we secondly delivered are,
From future sorrowes, and calamities,
The godly perish and are ta'ne away   *Esay.*57.1.
From ill to come, as *Esay* testifies.   130
And thus God cut off *Jeroboams* sonne,   1*King.*14.13.
Because he saw some good in him begun.

---

es 115–20. **Argia…Death:** The name "Argia" is taken from Argos, the chief seat of Hera's
no's) worship, and here applied to her priestess Cydippe. When oxen were not available,
dippe's sons Biton and Cleobis dragged their mother's chariot to Hera's temple; she asked
ra to reward them with the greatest boon possible for mortals, and they were given painless
d swift death in sleep. In Herodotus (1.31) Solon relates the story without giving the
ther's name.

We thirdly are, by *Death* exempt from sinne,
And freed from bondage of inthralled woe,
'Tis true, that life's the blessing of the Lord,
But yet by it sinne doth increase and grow.
And sinne is but the of-spring of the Devill,
Then blest is he, whom *Death* frees from this evill.

To some the Lord in mercie graunteth space,
For true repentance of committed sinne,
And reformation of those evill wayes,
Which through corruption they have walked in;
And other some, who sinne as earst before,
He takes away, that they may sinne no more.

Death Corporall in fine is as a dore,
Through which our soules doe passe without delay
Into those joyes, which cannot be conceiv'd;
This truth is proved plaine, where *Christ* doth say,
Luke 23.43. *To day thou shalt be with mee* to that theefe,
Which at last gaspe did beg his soules reliefe.

What is this world, if ballanced with heaven;
Earths glorie fades, but heavenly joyes indure,
This life is full of sicknesse, want, and woe;
But life through *Christ* hath no disease to cure.
In heaven there is no maladie or paine,
But melodie, true comfort to maintaine.

There Saints are Crown'd with matchlesse majestie,
Invested with eternall roabes of glorie;
There Sunne doth shine, and suffers no eclips,
Earths chiefest joyes are vaine, and transitorie.
Unconstant, fading, fickle, and unsure,
But heavens pleasures permanent endure.

There is no penurie, or choaking care
For present time, or the succeeding morrow;
But there are riches without toyle attain'd;   165
Myrth without mourning, solace without sorrow.
Peace without perill, plentie without want,
Where without asking, God doth all things grant.

The eye of man hath never yet beheld,   *1.Cor.*2.9.
Nor hath his eare atteined once to heare,   170
Ne yet his heart conceiv'd, or understood
The joyes prepar'd, and purchas'd for the deare
And chosen Children of our heavenly Father,
Who doth his sheepe into one sheepe-fould gather.

And as our soules possesse true happinesse,   175
So shall our mortall bodies vile and base,
Be rais'd immortall by the power of Christ,   *Phil.*3.21.
And with our soules enjoy a glorious place,
That re-united they may joyne in one,
To sing the praises of the *Corner-Stone*.   180 *Ephes.*2.20.

The day of *Death,* saith *Salomon* the Wise,
(Which paradox the Godly approbate)
Is better then the day that one is borne;   *Eccles.*7.3.
For *Death* conducts us to a blisse-full state.
'Tis *Lazars* friend, though it seeme *Dives* foe,   185
But life inducts us to a world of woe.

The Mariner, which doth assay to passe
The raging seas into some forraine land,

---

e 180. **Corner-Stone:** Christ.

e 182. **approbate:** approve.

e 185. **Lazars friend…Dives foe:** See Luke 16:19–31 for the parable of the begger Lazarus
the rich man, whose conditions are reversed after death. Dives, from the Latin for "rich," is
n translated as a proper name.

Desireth much to have his voyage ended,
And to arrive upon the solid sand.
All creatures with desire doe seeke for rest,
After they have with labour beene opprest.

The Pilgrim, which a journey undertakes,
Feeding his fancie with exoticke sights,
Deemes not his way much irkesome to his foot;
Because his paine is mixed with delights.
For 'tis his joy to thinke upon that day,
When he shall see the period of his way.

Men are as Saylors in this irksome life,
Who at the haven alwayes cast their eye,
As Pilgrims wandring in a uncouth land.
Then who is he, that will not wish to dye?
And he whom God by *Death* doth soonest call,
Is in my minde the happiest wight of all.

When *Simeon* had embraced in his armes,
His Lord, whom he had waited long to see,
He of his Saviour instantly desir'd
Luke 2.29.   A *nunc dimittis,* that he might be free
From bitter bondage of unpleasant life,
Where flesh and spirit alwayes are at strife.

By their Contraries things may best be seene,
Jet makes the Ivorie most white appeare,
'Tis darknesse which doth manifest the light,
And sicknesse makes us value health most deare.
Lifes miserie doth best make knowne the gaine,
And freedome, which by *Death* we doe obtaine.

Line 208. **nunc dimittis:** dismissal from life. Simeon's cry, "Now lettest thou thy ser⟨v⟩
depart" (Luke 2:29) begins with these words in the Latin (Vulgate) Bible.

Consider then the evils of this life,
Whose pleasures are as honie mixt with gall,
Or bankes of flowers, which cover lurking snakes,
Snares to intrap, and blocks whereat some fall.   220
What wise-man then of them will reck'ning make,
Or wish to live for fading pleasures sake?

It were some motive to induce delight,
In living long, if life would certaine last,
But *Infancie* and *Childhood* scarce are seene,   225
Before that both of them are overpast.
Juventus sodeinly doth flie away,
Adoloscency makes but little stay.

Virilitie doth not continue long,
Old-age is short and hastens to an end,   230
Our longest life and pleasure is but briefe,
Thus tedious griefes on every age attend.
Which like to sable clouds eclips our sunne,
And makes our glasse of life with sorrow run.

Consider man in his abridged time,   235
What pricking perill he therein doth beare;
Youth is incumbred with untimely harmes,
Continuall care doth *Middle-age* out-weare.
Old-age is testie, subject unto griefe,
Diseases steale upon it as a theefe.   240

The bodie is in danger (every part)
Of hurt, disease, and losse of sense, and lym,
Auditus unto deafenesse subject is,

---

227. **Juventus:** youth.

229. **Virilitie:** manhood, maturity.

243. **Auditus:** hearing. The Latin names for sight, taste, smell, and touch follow.

Visus of blindnesse, or of being dym,
Gustus of savours, bitter, tart, and sowre,
Olfactus unto loathsome stinks each houre.

Tactus is subject to benummednesse,
Our goods to spoyle by theeves, or sodeyne fire,
Good name is lyable to false reports,
Invective obtrectations, fruites of ire;
Our kindred and acquaintance subject are
To like mishap, which falleth to our share.

Our soule in danger is of vice and errour,
Our bodie subject to imprisonment,
To hurt by beasts, as horses and the like,
Or else to spoyle by creatures virulent;
Which with their stings doe give untimely wound,
Or else to squatts and bruises on the ground.

Those dewes, which *Sol* attracteth from the earth,
Prove most pernicious when they doe descend,
To number all the evills of this life,
May have beginning, but can finde no end.
For new enormities, new plagues procure,
'Tis just to scourge, where love cannot allure.

What course, or trade of life, is free from griefe?
Or what condition voyd of all annoy?
To live in office, trouble is our lot,

Line 250. **obtrectations:** detractions, slanders, calumnies (from Latin, *obtrectare, OED*).

Line 256. **spoyle...virulent:** destruction by poisonous creatures.

Line 258. **squatts:** wounds caused by a heavy fall (*OED*).

Lines 259–60. **dewes...descend:** The dews that evaporate into the skies may descend
storms and floods; readers would no doubt think of Noah's Flood (Gen. 6–8).

Line 264. **just...allure:** God justly sends such scourges when humans do not respond to
acts of love.

Line 267. **office:** in some public role or place.

To live at home is uncouth without joy:
To worke in field is toylesome, full of paine,
At sea are feares, in traffique little gaine.   270

In journey jeopardie doth us attend,
In marriage griefe and care oppresse the minde,
The single life is solitarie, vaine;
The rich can little joy in riches finde;
For having much, his care must watch his wealth,   275
From secret pilfring, and from open stealth.

If poverty be our appointed lot,
Our griefe is great, reliefe and comfort small,
We must endure oppression, suffer wrong,
The weake in wrestling goeth to the wall: 280
If we be bit, we cannot bite againe,
If rich men strike, we must their blow sustaine.

If we be eminent in place of note,
Then stand we as a marke for envies dart,
Conjecture censures our defect of worth,   285
Inquirie doth anatomize each part,
And if our reputation be but small,
Contempt and scorne doth us and ours befall.

The infant from the wombe into the world
Comes crying, by the which it doth presage   290
The paines, and perils, it must undergoe,
In childe-hood, man-hood, and decreped age,
He that most knowes this life, least doth it love,
Except affliction may affection move.

---

e 268. uncouth: unpleasant, unattractive (*OED*).
e 270. traffique: business.
e 280. The weake...wall: a proverb, often rendered, "the weakest is thrust to the wall." See
ey, W185.

Mans life on earth is like a Ship at Sea,
Tost on the waves of troubles to and fro,
Assayl'd by pirates, crost by blustring windes,
Where rockes of ruine menace overthrow.
Where stormes molest, and hunger pincheth sore,
Where *Death* doth lurke at every Cabbin dore.

Yet some afflictions in this irkesome life,
God doth in mercie to his Children send,
Thereby to weane them from the love of that,
Which is but noysome, and will soone have end.
Col. 3.2. That so their *liking may be set above*,
Upon those pleasures which shall never move.

*Phil.*1.23. Which made the Chosen vessell of the Lord,
That he might be with Christ, desire to *die*,
*Job.*6.8.9. And *Job* to wish his dayes were at an end,
Because his life was nought but miserie.
The godly man is tyred with his breath,
And findes no rest, till he be free by *Death*.

What then is life that it should be desir'd?
Or what advantage by it doth man winne?
Is not this world a net to snare the soule?
Doe not long livers multiplie their sinne?
Is not this life a mappe of miserie,
The quite contrarie of tranquilitie.

For though the seeming pleasures of this life
Doe cause us love it, yet the paines may move
Us to contemne the bait, which hides the hooke,
And rather loath, then either like or love,
A path of Ice, where footing is unsure,
Or bitter pills, though guilded to allure.

But some (who live as *Dives* did) may say,   325
That life is sweet, and comfort doth afford,
That there are few whom sicknesse doth arrest,
But wish most earnestly to be restor'd.
That *Hezekiah* wept when he heard tell,   1.*King*.20.3.
That God would have him bid the world farewell.   330

As also *David* to the Lord did say,
Let my soule live, that it may praise thee still;   Psal.119.175.
And Christ did pray, his *Cup* might from him passe,   Luke 22.42.
If so it were his holy Fathers will:
But *Hezekiah* wept, because that yet   335
He had no issue on his throne to sit.

And *Davids* wish from reason did proceed;
For he was then perplexed with his foe,
Who would with exultation have affirm'd,
That God in wrath had wrought his overthrow.   340
And of Christs prayer this was the reason why,
Because he was a cursed *Death* to die.   Gal.3.13.

When godly men doe dread the sight of *Death*,
Their fearefulnesse it is but natures errour,
The spirit's readie, but the flesh is weake,   345 Mat.26.41.
Assisting grace will mitigate their terror.
Yet some mens feare doth issue from mistrust,
That they shall never shine among the just.

The conscience of whose life in sinne mis-led,
At sight of *Death* doth make them trembling stand,   350
And like *Belshatsar* change their wonted lookes,   Dan.5.6.
Because that their destruction is at hand.

---

e 341. Christs prayer: In the Garden of Gethsemane Christ prayed to be spared, if
ssible, his imminent passion and death, "Father, if it be possible, let this cup pass from me"
att. 26:39). See lines 333–34.

For when that God o're them gives *Death* full power,
Grave takes their bodies, hell their soules devoure.

They know that sinne deserves eternall *Death;*
And therefore feare when they depart from hence,
And that their Lampe of life is quite extinct,
Their pleasures shall conclude, and paines commence.
The worme of *Conscience* gnawes so in their brest,
As makes their terrour not to be exprest.

*Num.*23.10.   And then (too late) with *Balam* they desire,
(When they perceive their latter end draw nie)
That they the righteous may assimilate
In their departure, and like them may die.
But holy life is that portendeth blisse,
He that lives well can never die amisse.

That man which lives a sanctifyed life,
Yet doth not die with outward peace and rest,
Through conflicts had with Sathan and his lusts;
Judge not amisse of him, whom God hath blest.
In leading by the gate of hell to joy,
Where he shall be exempt from all annoy.

For sometimes 'tis the lot of wicked men,
Which in impietie their life have led,
To outward view to leave this world in peace,
Without so much as strugling on their bed.
1. *Sam.* 25.37.   The *Death* of *Nabal* who so noteth well,
Shall finde that many passe like stones to hell.

*Gen.*40.13.19.   *Death* is the messenger of weale and woe,
Like *Joseph,* which foretold of dignitie,
That *Pharaoh* on his Butler would bestow,
But to the Baker fatall miserie.

He did predict should sodeinly ensue,
Which, as he said, did quickly fall out true.

Unto the faithfull, *Death* doth tydings bring   385
Of life, of favour, and eternall rest,
How they from out the prison of this world,
In which with griefes they have beene sore opprest,
Shall be receiv'd through Christs eternall love
To live for ever with their God above.   390

For though that *Death* considered in it selfe
Be fearefull, and doth many terrors bring,
Yet unto them there is no cause of dread;
For by Christs *Death* grim *Mors* hath lost it sting.
That as a toothlesse Snake no hurt can doe,   395
No more can *Death* procure the godly woe.

The sting of *Death* the Scripture sayth is *sinne*,   1.*Cor.*15.56.
Christs powerfull *Death* hath tooke *Deaths* power away,
That by the merit of his Conquering word;
To *Death* and Hell we may with boldnesse say,   400   *Hosea* 13.14.
Death where's thy sting, Hell where's thy victorie?
In Christ we live maugre thy tyrannie.   1.*Cor.*15.55.

The godly onely comfort finde in *Death*,
They view the end, and not regard the way,
And with the eye of faith they see, that God   405
Intends more good to them, then earth can pay:
And though *to die* they dare not supplicate,
Yet for their dissolution they doe waite.

---

e 394. **Mors:** Roman god of death.
e 402. **maugre:** despite.

So that if *Death* arrest them unawares,
Yet can it not them unprepared finde,
And if with respite they depart this world,
Their wel-led-life doth consolate their minde,
And makes them welcome *Death* with joy of heart;
'Tis happie newes that they from life must part.

But to the wicked *Death* brings word of *Death;*
For why to them it hath not lost it sting:
It is but the exordium of their woes,
And as a Goalor doth from Prison bring
Their guiltie soules, to suffer for their sinne
Those paines which end not, though they doe begin.

Within them terror doth affright their mindes,
Above them they the face of justice see,
Beneath them horrour doth affront their sight,
About them ugly Devils readie bee,
With watchfull eyes, most willing without grudge,
To execute the pleasure of the Judge.

Death takes them as it findes them, and forthwith
It doth present them, as it doth them take,
Unto the Lord, who censures their deserts,
As they are found, when they appearance make.
And as they are adjudged, so they must,
For ever under-goe their sentence just.

Mortalitie is Gods exact decree,
Which as the deluge of his kindled ire,
Hath overwhelmed with a dying life
Decaying man, whose state doth still require,

Line 416. **For why:** because.

Line 417. **exordium:** introduction to an oration or formal treatise.

Line 425. **grudge:** reluctance.

And pregnantly induce to thinke on *Death*,
Ere it obstruct the passage of his breath.

Three motives moving man to meditate
On *Death*, ere *Death*, I briefely will declare; 440 *Psal.*89.48.
First the *Necessitie* that men *must die*, *Deut.*31.14.
By which they are forewarned to prepare,
Against that time, when they *must* goe from hence,
This strict *Oportet* will with none dispence.

Those daily objects man doth speculate, 445
Present unto his thought, that he *must die;*
For all things in this world declare and shew,
That man is subject to *Mortalitie;*
Those vegetives, which bud and spring out most,
Doth *Hyems* kill, and cut away with frost. 450

The elements must be dissolv'd with heate, *1.Pet.*3.10.
The *Macrocosmus* it must passe away,
And man the *Microcosmus* needs *must die*, *Luke* 21.33.
Both young and old *must* goe to *Golgotha*.
Faire buildings levell with the ground must lye, 455
And strongest Citties come to nullitie.

The *Medes* and *Persians* did their lawes confirme *Dan.*6.15.
So strongly, that they could not altred bee,
And this appointment *all men once must die*, *Heb.*9.27.

---

e 444. **Oportet:** necessity, literally "It is necessary."

e 445. **speculate:** view.

e 450. **Hyems:** hiems, winter (Latin), often personified, as here.

e 452. **Macrocosmus:** universe.

e 454. **Golgotha:** the place where Jesus was crucified, meaning, "place of a skull" (Matt.
33).

e 457. **Medes and Persians:** laws understood to be unalterable. See Esther 1:19, "Now, O
g, establish the decree, and sign the writing, that it be not changed, according to the law of
Medes and Persians, which altereth not."

Is as infallible, as their decree.

2.Sam.14.14.

We needs must die, to pay what God doth lend,
Life had beginning, and *must* have an end.

From earth man came, to dust he *must* returne,
This is the descant of *Deaths* fatall dittie,
All men are mortall, therefore *must* they die,

Heb.13.14.

And *Paul* sayth, *Here is no abiding Cittie.*
Mans dayes consume like wax against the Sunne,

Job 7.6.

And as a Weavers shuttle swiftly runne.

That thing, which may bee, may be doubted of,
And as a thing uncertaine passe neglected;
But things that *must* be, greater heed require,
And of necessitie *must* bee expected.
Then thinke on *Death,* ere *Death,* for truth doth show,
That *Death must* come, but when we may not know.

The second motive mooving thought of *Death,*
Is the impartialitie of it,
Respecting neither persons, age, or sexe,
By bribes sinister it doth none acquit;
Friends nor intreaties can no whit prevaile,
Where *Death* arrests it will admit no Bayle.

What is become of *Absolom* the faire?
David the Victor, *Salomon* the wise?
Cressus the worldly rich, *Dives* the wretch?
Sampson the strong, that was bereft of eyes?

Line 464. **descant:** a variation on the chief melody or theme (*OED*).

Lines 467–68. **Mans...runne:** proverbial sayings.

Line 483. **Cressus:** Croesus, last king of the Lydians (6th century), a byword for we ("Rich as Croesus"). The biblical personages are also identified by qualities taken to characteristic of them: See 2 Sam. 14:25, 1 Sam. 18:7, 2 Chron. 1:9–12, Luke 16:24, Juc 16:15–17.

From these, and more then these, with whetted knife,   485
Death hath cut off the silver thread of life.

It is hereditarie unto all,
Lazarus dead, Dives must also die,   *Luke* 16.22.
Passe from his downe-bed to his bed of dust,
And untill doomes day in earths bowels lye.   490
Death scatters that, which life had carking got,
And casts on youthfull yeares old ages lot.

Like *Jehues* shaft it spares not *Jorams* heart,   2.*King* 9.24.
But makes Kings subject to its awelesse power.
David must yeeld to tread the beaten path,   495
When *Death* with open mouth meanes to devoure.   1.*King* 2.2.
And having changed corps to dust, who then
Can well distinguish Kings from other men?

The greatest Monarch of earths Monarchie,
Whom God with worldly honours highly blest,   500
Deaths Beesome from this life hath swept away,
Their stories Epilogue is *Mortuus est.*   *Gen.*5.5.
For *Death* to all men dissolution brings,
Yea, the *Catastrophe* it is of Kings.

Great *Alexander* Conquer'd many Lands,   505
And savage Creatures he bereft of breath;
But in the Records of his famous acts,

ᴸᵉ 491. **carking:** with anxious care, labor, pains (*OED*).

ᴸᵉ 494. **awelesse:** awesome.

ᴸᵉ 501. **Beesome:** besom, a broom made of twigs tied together (*OED*).

ᴸᵉ 502. **Mortuus est:** He is dead.

ᴸᵉ 504. **Catastrophe:** the turning point of a tragedy, casting the hero down to destruction
ᵈ (usually) death.

ᴸᵉ 505. **Great Alexander:** Alexander the Great (356–323 B.C.) was famous for conquests of
ᵉᵉce, Egypt, and much of Asia Minor, including Persia and Babylon.

It is not writ, that he did Conquer *Death*.
The stoutest souldiour fitted for the field,
Maugre his might to *Death* his life must yeeld.

Methushelah, one of the longest livers,
Could not escape the peircing dart of *Death,*
But when the sand out of his glasse was runne,
Mors stopt the passage of his vitall breath.
Death from the stately throne to grave dejects,
No more the Prince then Peasant it respects.

It doth dissolve the knot by friendship knit,
From *David* it takes *Jonathan* away,
And Children of their Parents it bereaves,
Parents their Children must not have for aye.
Without respect of any or remorce,
It workes the husband's, and his wifes divorce.

'Tis so impartiall, that it spareth none,
But doth surprize the rich as well as poore,
It was not *Tullies* learned eloquence,
That could perswade *Death* to passe by his dore.
Nor is it wealth or prowesse that can tame,
*Gen.*3.19.   *Deaths* vigour, for it sends men whence they came.

The third and last is the *uncertaintie*
Of *Deaths* approach, as *when* or at what time,
It will arrest us, whether in old age,
Or our Virilitie and youthfull prime.
The which must cause continuall thought of *Death,*
That unawares it may not stop our breath.

Line 511. **Methushelah:** Methuselah, who lived 969 years (Gen. 5:27).

Line 518. **David...Jonathan:** They were bosom friends and soul-mates, the primary bib
exemplar of friendship. See 1 Sam. 18:1, 3.

Line 520. **for aye:** forever.   Line 525. **Tullies:** Cicero's.

Time turnes the heavens in a certaine course,   535
The Storke and Crane appoynted seasons know,   *Jer.*8.7.
The starres their constant motions doe observe,
Tides have their times to ebbe and over-flow.
Mans fickle state doth onely rest unsure
Of certaine course, and season to endure.   540

The Tenant thinkes upon that date of time,
Which will his lease of house or land expire;
But of the end or *punctum* of this life,
Whereof we have no lease, who doth inquire?
We in this life are Tenants but at will,   545
God onely knowes the time we must fulfill.

The Preter time, which is alreadie past,
Was ours, but never will be so againe;
The Future time perhaps shall not be ours,
To make account thereof is therefore vaine;   550
The instant time which present we injoy
Is onely ours to mannage and imploy.

I make no doubt but many men would mourne,
If they exactly knew their finall day
Should be within a yeare of present time,   555
Yet now with mirth they passe their time away;
When as perhaps they shall not live one houre,
Nay in a moment, *Death* may them devoure.

Some tender Infants in their Cradle die,
Like blooming blossomes blowne from off the tree;   560
Davids young sonne *must die,* it is decreed,   2.*Sam.*12.18.
That length of dayes he shall not live to see.
Thus greedie *Death* plucks buds from off the tree,
When fruits mature grow and ungath'red bee.

---

ke 543. **punctum:** period.   Line 547. **Preter:** past.

There is no man on earth that can foretell,
Where Death, or in what place will us select,
Abroad, at home, in cittie, or the field,
It is *Uncertaine,* that we may expect
Deaths comming alwayes, and in every place,
To make compleate the currant of our race.

The manner of *Deaths* comming, *How* 'twill be,
God hath conceal'd to make us vigilant.
Some die by sicknesse, others by mishap,
Some die with surfeit, other some with want:
Some die by fire, some perish by the Sword,
Some drown'd in Water swim unto the Lord.

Pope *Adrian* was stifeled with a Gnatt,
Old *Anacreon* strangled with a Grape,
A little hayre did choake great *Fabius,*
Saphira could not sodeine *Death* escape.
Into this life we all but one way came,
But divers wayes we goe out of the same.

If God from perill did not us protect,
Our daily food might stop our vitall breath,
The things we neither doubt, nor feare, may prove

Line 577. **Pope Adrian:** Hadrian IV (d. 1157). John Bale, *The Pageant of the Popes,* trans. J
(London, 1574), reports that he was punished by God in this manner a few days after
excommunicated the Holy Roman Emperor: "when he came to a certaine springe of water
dranke thereof, and forthwith a flye did enter his mouth, and did cleave to his throate in s
sort that no art of the Physitions could get it away, and so he was choked therewith, and d
therof" (fol. 97v).

Line 578. **Anacreon:** Greek lyric poet (c. 560–480 B.C.) who sang of love and wine, repu
to be a consummate voluptuary. Pliny, *Historia Naturalis* 7.7, reports that he choked on a gr
stone.

Line 579. **Fabius:** Pliny, *Historia Naturalis* 7.7, also records the death "by a single hair i
draught of milk" of "the praetor Fabius Senator," and draws a moral about the fragility
human life.

Line 580. **Saphira:** Sapphira, wife of Ananias who, like her husband, was struck dead
punish their lies in withholding money promised to God (Acts 5:1–10).

The instruments of an untimely *Death*.
And in a moment worke our lives decay,
When we least thinke upon our ending day.

'Tis God omniscient which doth onely know
The time of life, that man on earth must live,   590
At his appoyntment *Moses must goe die*,   *Deut.*32.50.
Who bounds and limmit unto time doth give:
Man happen may to aske *Where, When,* and *How,*
Death will surprize, but God sayth *Thus, here, now.*

Of lifes decay man information hath,   595
From certaine *monitors*, which Usher *Death;*
The first whereof proclaimes th' uncertaintie
Of time determin'd for mans use of breath.
The second doth discover miserie.
The third inevitable certaintie.   600

The first of these is sodeine casualtie,
Which doth suggest that *Death* may doubtfull be,
The second sicknesse, which with irksome groanes
Declares, that *Death* may grievous be to thee.
Thirdly old-age this rule doth verifie,   605
Young men may faile, but aged men must die.

It therefore is most requisite for those,
That wish to be upright in judgement found,
Not by their workes, but for their Saviours meed,
To thinke they alwayes heare the last trump sound,   610
That they their soules in readinesse may make:
For when *Death* comes 'twill no excuses take.

---

es 601–2. **sodeine...be:** sudden or unexpected casualties indicate that the time of death is
certain.

e 609. **meed:** grace, gift.

*Deut.*32.29.   *Jehovah* by his *Utinam* doth shew
His great desire, that men should have respect
To *understand* and thinke upon their end,
Which want of wisedome causeth them neglect.
For surely where the Lord doth knowledge give,
Men live and learne to *die,* and *die* to live.

To entertaine a Legate from a King
In costly manner, many will prepare;
Yet *Death* that comes from him, that's King of Kings,
Welcome to bid, there are but few that care;
*Eccl.*11.3.   But *as the tree doth fall, so shall it lye,*
And men must rise to Judgement as they *die.*

That thing, which at all seasons may be done,
When ever done, is not done out of season;
A daily expectation of that guest,
Which any time may come proceeds from reason.
Jerusalem her latter end forgot,
And therefore desolation was her lot.

Invading *Mors* without remorse devoures,
And if we be not arm'd ere it assault,
We shall be foyled ere we can be arm'd;
If we be taken tardie 'tis our fault.
For sith 'tis certaine, *Mors* will surely strike,
We must expect *Deaths* poyson-pointed pyke.

That unawares we may not be surpriz'd,
But readie to receive that fatall blowe,
Which cannot be resisted when it comes,
No more then force of flouds which overflow.
Premeditation is the best defence
Against this foe, which will with none dispence.

Line 613. **Utinam:** exclamation, "If only," "Would that."

For from continuall thought of *Deaths* assault,
Doe sundry speciall benefits arise,
Carelesse securitie it first prevents,   645
Wherewith our ghostly foe doth blind our eyes;
And by the which he makes us quite forget,
That there's a Centre in our Circle set.

By thought of *Death* (in second place) we gaine
Acquaintance, with our foe afore our fight,   650
Expected dangers loose their greatest force.
Pauls dying daily put false feare to flight.   1.*Cor.*15.31.
'Those faces, which at first have ugly hew,
'Grow into liking through their often view.

Thirdly by thought of *Death,* ere life decay,   655
We shall contemne this world and hold it vaine,
Into the which we nothing brought at first,
Nor from it can we carrie ought againe.   1.*Tim.*6.7.
As also know whil'st on this Sea we floate,
We are but strangers, from our home remote.   660

The *Dove,* which *Noah* sent from forth the *Arke,*   *Gen.*8.9.
Could finde no rest, till shee return'd againe;
Nor can the faithfull, till they goe to Christ,
True rest and quiet without griefe obtaine:
Heaven is the haven of the faithfull wight,   665
Christ's love the object of their soules delight.

The soule of *David* panted after God,   *Psal.*42.1.
And thirsted oft his presence to obtaine;
The father of the faithfull liv'd in tents,   *Heb.*11.9.

---

e 646. **ghostly foe:** spiritual foe, the Devil.
e 648. **Centre in our Circle:** i.e., our center is properly God.
e 665. **wight:** person.
e 669. **father of the faithfull:** Abraham.

And stranger-like in *Canaan* did remaine.
That he might no where settle his abode,
But in the Cittie of the living God.

Fourthly, premeditation of our *Death*,
Doth cause us crucifie our sinfull lust,
Gal.5.24. And by the spirit mortifie the flesh,
That soule may live when bodie turnes to *dust;*
And makes us know that costly roabes and meate,
Doe decke and nourish food for Wormes to eate.

Fifthly, the thought of our decease by *Death*,
Doth move us seriously to waigh in minde,
How that our first materiall was but earth;
Job.7.7. That life is short, unconstant as the Winde:
Like mist and dew, which Sunne doth drive away,
Job.9.26. Or swift as Eagles hasting to their pray.

*1.Pet.*1.24. Man is in sacred Writ compar'd to grasse,
Which flourishing to day sends forth its flowre,
With'ring at night, is cast into the fire,
Of short persistance, like an Aprill showre.
For who so now perceives the Sunne to shine,
His life is done before that it decline.

*Psal.*102.3. Our dayes consume and passe away like smoake,
Like Bavens blaze soone kindled, soone extinct,
Job.9.26. Or like a Ship which swiftly slides the Sea,
Uncertaine, fickle, irkesome, and succinct.
Recite I all the fading types I can,
Yet none so momentanie as is man.

Line 692. **Bavens:** bavin, a bundle of brushwood or light underwood (*OED*).
Line 696. **momentanie:** lasting but for a moment, ephemeral (*OED*).

Unto a shadow *Job* doth life compare,   *Job.*8.9.
Which when the bodie moves, doth vanish quite,
To vanitie, and likewise to a dreame,   *Job.*20.8.
Whereof we have an hundred in one night.   700
David's resembling life unto a span,   *Psal.*39.5.
Doth shew the short continuance of man.

If happinesse consist in length of dayes,
An Oke more happie then a man appeares;
So doth the *Elephant,* and sturdie *Stagge,*   705
Which commonly doe live two hundred yeares:
But mortall man, as *Moses* doth unfould,   *Psal.*90.10.
If he live fourescore yeares is counted old.

When *Xerxes* with ten hundred thousand men
Attempted warre, his eyes did showre forth teares;   710
To thinke, not one of those, whom he imploy'd,
Should be alive within one hundred yeares.
For *Adams* heyres ingaged doe remaine
To pay, what he receiv'd, and lost againe.

The day wherein we first behold the light,   715
Begins our *Death,* for life doth daily fade,
Our day of *Death* begins our happie life,
We are in danger, till our debt is paid.
Life is but lent, we owe it to the Lord,
When 'tis demanded, it must be restor'd.   720

A false imagination of long life
Made *Dives* sing a *requiem* to his soule,   *Luke* 12.19.
Inlarge his Barnes, disport, and make good cheare,
Till just *Jehovah* did his thoughts controwle.

---

es 709–12. **Xerxes...yeares:** Xerxes, king of Persia (c. 485–465 B.C.), wept when he
ved his massive army and fleet gathered at Abydos for his war against Greece, because they
ıld all be dead in a hundred years (Herodotus, 7.41–46).

Who calls him *foole,* and quells his fond delight,
By threat'ning judgement to befall that night.

Sixthly, the thought of *Deaths* most sure approach,
Doth move contrition for our preter sinne,
And workes restraint of present ill desires,
Inspiring constant purpose to begin,
A faithfull life by Gods assisting grace,
That to his glory we may runne our race.

Lastly, premeditation of our *Death,*
Induceth us to commendable care,
For setling and disposing our estate
To those, whom we intend shall have a share,
That when we are departed from this life,
Our goods may prove no coales to kindle strife.

Esay 38.1.

When *Hezekiah Judahs* King was sicke,
And at the entrie of *Deaths* dore did lye,
The Prophet *Esay* came to him, and sayd,
Put thou thy house in order, thou must die;
Which paradigma plainely doth ingrave
That 'tis a dutie God himselfe doth crave.

Neglect of which disturbs us at our end,
When we should be exempt from worldly care,
When doubt of who shall reape what we have sowne
Distracts our thoughts, and doth our peace impaire;
Withdrawing our affections from above,
Where we and no where els should fixe our love.

Line 741. **Esay:** Isaiah.
Line 743. **paradigma:** a lesson, warning (Greek).

Unto that place prepar'd for Gods elect
Afore the world, the Lord conduct us still,
And grant that we the measure of our dayes,
To his good pleasure may on earth fulfill;
That when wee to our period doe attaine,   755
We may with Christ in glory ever raigne.

Amen.

Lord Jesus come quickly.

FINIS.

Faults escaped in Printing.

Page 59. line 280. for *perceiving* read *pearcing*.
Page 67. line 170. for *attended* read *atteined*.
Page 72. line 310. for *naught* read *nought*.

Errata list. Page numbers have been changed to conform to the present edition.

Appendix

A Contemporary Response to Speght's *Mouzell:* Marginalia in the Yale Copy

e Beinecke Library at Yale holds a copy of Rachel Speght's *Mouzell Melastomus* (Ih Sp 33 617m) containing some eighty-seven manu-
pt annotations in a contemporary hand.[1] Such extensive commen-
y is most unusual in the period: it provides an example of Jacobean
der response in which a male annotator reacted to Speght's authorial
ims and protofeminist arguments and worked out strategies for deal-
; with them. The intertextual dialogue of text and margins affords a
:inating insight into contemporary cultural attitudes and gender
ıes.

The annotator's identity is uncertain, but I think the most likely
ıdidate is Swetnam himself, rising to Rachel's challenge to answer her
ırges (page 33) and making notes of likely rejoinders. One piece of
dence is Constantia Munda's report that she heard he was preparing
growl back at Speght.[2] Another is the fact that the annotator knows
etnam's text very well and offers to clarify his positions or intentions
meaning in several passages.[3] More revealing, perhaps, he explains
ıt one of the grammatical gaffes Rachel derided (#75) was in fact a
nter's error, and on at least one occasion (#78), he undertakes to
:ak for Swetnam. Unfortunately, I found no examples of Swetnam's
ıd for comparison.

Alternatively, the annotator may be another polemicist who made
tes in Speght's text preparatory to answering her and defending Swet-
m. His occasional assumption of a "third-party" stance, as of one
ıling (though hardly evenhandedly) between the two parties might,

---

See Cis van Heertum, "A Hostile Annotation of Rachel Speght's *A Mouzell for Melastomus* 17)," *English Studies* 6 (1987): 490–96, and Lewalski, "Female Text, Male Reader ponse: Contemporary Marginalia in Rachel Speght's *A Mouzell for Melastomus* (1617)," in *resenting Women in the English Renaissance,* ed. Claude J. Summers and Ted-Larry Pebworth lumbia: University of Missouri Press, 1996), forthcoming.

See above, page xx.

E.g., #2, #67, #68, #71, #76, #83; I have numbered the annotations below, for easy rence.

but need not, suggest as much.[4] Also, these marginalia do not con
obvious verbal echoes of Swetnam's *Araignment* and their tone se
more irate and contemptuous of women than Swetnam's tract does.
of course Swetnam might well strike out in a harsher and more derc
tory vein when answering the pointed attacks of a particular woman

It seems unlikely that the annotator is some casual reader move
rage by Speght's tract. The sheer number of annotations argues aga
that, as does, more forcefully, the writer's intimate knowledge not c
of Swetnam's work but also of Speght's circumstances: that she
"priest daughter"—something she does not reveal in her tract—
that she had the reputation of being a sensible and discerning wor
before publishing this book.[5]

If these marginalia are notes toward an intended response to Spe
by Swetnam or another writer, they exemplify an early stage of the p
cess by which early modern controversialists often engaged with offe
ing texts, answering them page by page, detail by detail. But if writt
this answer was probably not published. Speght would almost certai
have singled out any such full-scale attack when she refers in the epi
to *Mortalities Memorandum* to the variety of opinions and censures
tract elicited. Possibly the annotator or the publisher came to beli
that such an attack on a well-connected young woman of good repu
tion might backfire.

Whoever he was, the annotator's strategies for dealing with the f
Englishwoman to publish a serious polemic defending women
familiar enough—early versions of what have proved to be quite du
ble methods for trying to keep subversive women in their place. Seve
rejoinders condescend to Rachel's youth and female ignorance.[6] M
more are explicit sexual put-downs: puns on female genitalia, rude
erences to body parts or to sexual intercourse, double entendres, a
slurs on Rachel's chastity—attacks which take on special force si
they are directed against a known young unmarried woman, highly v

4. E.g., #12, #13.

5. See #73, #7.

6. See, e.g., #5, #74, #76.

rable to insinuations of unchastity and indecorum.[7] Other comments
erpret Rachel's biblically-grounded praises of marriage as evidence
t she, like all maids, desperately wants and needs a husband, and that
intends, moreover, to rule him.[8] At times the annotator picks up on
vord or phrase of Speght's to point to stereotypical female evils and
aknesses: women are vain, much marred, the cause of men's pains
d utter destruction.[9] The effect of all this is to make Rachel a partic-
r example of the stereotypical follies of the entire sex—ignorance,
akness, voracious sexual appetite, desire to dominate men, vanity,
seemly speech, shrewishness, propensity to sin.

Several notes respond to Speght's biblical citations and exegeses argu-
; women's excellence either by denying the relevance of her examples
else insisting that women have marred their original good creation by
and cosmetic artifice.[10] However, the annotator seldom engages
eght's reinterpretations of scripture; he simply reiterates conventional
sogynistic readings of Eve, or Solomon's wives, or Paul's advice not to
rry.[11] Her reading of the parable of the talents (#45) he dismisses
h a reference to Seneca's advice to teach by example not by precept,
an obvious effort to reinscribe female silence.

The annotations are reproduced below along with enough of
eght's text to clarify the intertextual dialogue. On a few occasions
ere a letter or word is blurred or was cropped when the text was
ound I record my guesses in square brackets. Words which the anno-
or underlined in Speght's text are underlined here: often they are the
ecise target of the response. I have numbered the annotations (in the
ht margin) for reference.

See, e.g., #16, #17, #20, #26, #27, #70, #81, #83.
See, e.g., #47, #48, #49, #50, #52, #54, #57, #58.
E. g., #10, #18, #31, #53.
  E. g., #29, #39, #44, #67, #68.
  E. g., #31, #33, #36, #37.

GHT'S *MOUZEL*	MARGINALIA

LE PAGE EPIGRAPH Proverbs 26.5

wer a foole according to his foolishnesse, lest
ee wise in his owne conceit.

	Shee that calleth her booke foole is worthy to bee punished with Hell fire. 1

E EPISTLE DEDICATORIE

ng the *Bayter of Women* hath opened his
uth against noble as well as ignoble,
nst the rich as well as the poore.

	But not against good woemen of which there 2 are a few.

E PREFACE

m standing water, which soon putrifies,
no good fish be expected

	[Note crossed out and illegible] 3

ablably, no better streame can we looke,
uld issue from your idle corrupt braine,
n that whereto the ruffe of your fury (to
your owne words) hath moved you to
n the sluce.

	[Note crossed out and illegible] 4

r dealing wants so much discretion, that I
abt whether to bestow so good a name as
Dunce upon you: but Minority bids me
pe within my bounds; and therefore I
ie say unto you, that your corrupt Heart
railing Tongue, hath made you a fit scribe
the Divell.

	Shee cannot chuse butt maybe doe what she 5 can.

od had it beene for you to have put on that
zzell, which Saint *James* would have all
ristians to weare; *Speake not evill one of*
ther.

	Likewise it is sayd, revile not those that revile: 6 which muzzell would verie well have fitted your mouth in manie places of this booke.

this your hodge-podge of heathenish Sences, Similes, and Examples, you have set
h your selfe in your right colours, unto the
w of the world: and I doubt not but the
icious will account of you according to
r demerit: As for the Vulgar sort, which
e no more learning then you have shewed
our Booke, it is likely they will applaud
for your paines.

	You your selfe weare one of the Juditious: but 7 now by reason of your publique booke, not soe good as common.

for your *Bugge-beare* or advice unto
men, that whatsoever they doe thinke of
r Worke, they should conceale it, lest in
ding fault, they bewray their galled backes
he world; in which you allude to that
verbe, *Rubbe a galled horse, and he will*
ze: Unto it I answere by way of Apologie,
though every galled horse, being touched,

	Kickinge is a verie ill quallitie in anie horse: 8 which you can not cleare your feete of: for youre sowre wordes moove it against you. But a sound & good horse, and soe consequently a good woeman will neither kicke nor wince.

doth kicke; yet every one that kickes, is not galled: so that you might as well have said, that because burnt folks dread the fire, therfore none feare fire but those that are burnt.

Further, if your owne words be true, that you wrote with your hand, but not with your heart, then are you <u>an hypocrite in Print</u>: but it is rather to be thought that your Pen was the bewrayer of the abundance of your minde, and that this was but a little morter to dawbe up agayne the wall, which you intended to breake downe.

You should rather have absolved him th⸗ have given this harde sentence against for hee deal[s] with weomen, as weomen with theire children, to make them good are they loath to beate them, and manie t theire hands wilbee against theire hearts.

[crossed out line]
weomen be a wall, the wall is full of cr⸗ and needes much morter to mend it.

Butt sure you are a Devile incarnate, if heart went with your hande: and your to⸗ avouch it.

The revenge of your rayling Worke wee leave to Him, who hath appropriated vengeance unto himselfe, whose Pen-man hath included Raylers in the Catalogue of them, that shall not inherite Gods Kingdome, and your selfe unto the mercie of that just Judge, who is able to save and to destroy.

God have mercy on yea both; and make his servants; for sure neither booke hathe ter owner

Your undeserved friend, RACHEL SPEGHT

Kisse & bee freinds

DEDICATORY POEMS.
[First poem]
If <u>little</u> *David* that for *Israels* sake,
  esteemed neyther life nor limbe too deare,
In that he did adventure without dread,
  to cast at him, whom all the hoste did feare,
A stone, which brought *Goliah* to the ground,
Obtain'd applause with Songs and Timbrels
sound.

Neaver to little if olde enough.

Then let another <u>young</u> encombatant
  receive applause, and thankes, as well as
      hee:
For with an enemie to Women kinde,
  she hath encountred, as each wight may see:
And with the fruit of her industrious toyle,
To this <u>*Goliah*</u> she hath given the foyle.

Neaver to younge if bigg enough.

What? throwinge stones?
Give mee her arse.

mire her much I may, both for her age,
nd this her Mouzell for a blacke-mouth'd
  wight,
  praise her, and her worke, to that desert,
hich unto them belongs of equall right
nnot; onely this I say, and end,
ee is unto her Sex a faithfull friend.

Shee is to bee admired at for her muzzell. why   17
what manner of mouth hath shee, for that's
her muzzell.

Shee is? She is a desperate vanity   18
I'le warrant her, goe toe.

ned] PHILALETHES

[Changed to] Philogunes   19

cond poem]

ae that for his <u>Countrie</u> doth expose
imselfe unto the furie of his foe,
th merite praise and due respect of those,
or whom he did that perill undergoe:
en let the Author of this Mouzell true
ceive the like, of right it is her due.

Doth shee fight for her Cunt-rie.   20
for a puddinge as soone.

r she to <u>shield</u> her Sex from Slaunders Dart,
nd from invective obtrectation,
th ventured by force of Learnings Art,
n which she hath had education)
combate with him, which doth shame his
  Sex,
offring feeble women to perplex.

Shee must have a large sheilde to receive all   21
the darts that are shott at her whole sexe.

hird poem]

Virgin <u>young</u>, and of such tender age,
for encounter may be deemd too weake,

You dare not sweare for hir virginitie unlesse   22
you bee her servant: and then you dare doe
anie thinge.

ee having not as yet seene twenty yeares,
ough in <u>her carriage</u> older she appeares.

I have knowen those that have encounterd as   23
valiant men as this at raw fifteene and have
made them yeilde their weapon.

It seemes shee is of a good Carri-age.   24

r <u>wit and learning</u> in this present Worke,
ore praise doth merit, then my quill can
  write:
r <u>magnanimitie</u> deserves applaud,
ventring with a <u>fierie</u> foe to fight:
And now in fine, what shall I further say?
But that she beares the triumph quite away.

By my troath, noe.   25

Neither, unlesse hee bee a Philistine foe &   26
carries his fire in his tayle.

Thy mistress beares the prick & prizz away   27

MOUZELL FOR MELASTOMUS
oigraph from Proverbs 18:22]
  that findeth a wife, findeth a good thing,
 d receiveth favour of the Lord.

He that findeth a good wife.   28
["good" inserted above the line].

The worke of Creation being finished, this approbation thereof was given by God him-selfe, That *All was very good:* If All, then *Woman,* who, excepting man, is the most excellent creature under the Canopie of heaven.

It was verie good: but since the creation: v man hath mismade, & misform'd her si thats not verie good

Here the femall sexe is at variance about n for Jacob sayth, that woeman is the w creature under ye Sunn; Man only excep Rachel sayes that man is the most excell Oh excellent

To the first of these objections I answere; that Sathan first assailed the woman, because where the hedge is lowest, most easie it is to get over, and she being the weaker vessell was with more facility to be seduced.

The devill said, trust in himselfe too be weake, & tender. Sett the woeman to dec the man, shee is much more cunning deceive, then the devill.

And if *Adam* had not approved of that deed which *Eve* had done, and beene willing to treade the steps which she had gone, hee being her Head would have reproved her, and have made the commandement a bit to restraine him from breaking his Makers Injunction: For if a man burne his hand in the fire, the bellowes that blowed the fire are not to be blamed, but himselfe rather, for not being carefull to avoyde the danger: Yet if the bellowes had not blowed, the fire had not burnt;

Eve first threw herselfe into the fire, pulled Adam after her.

no more is woman simply to bee condemned for mans transgression: for by the free will, which before his fall hee enjoyed, hee might have avoyded, and beene free from beeing burnt, or singed with that fire which was kin-dled by Sathan, and blowne by *Eve.*

You may see by this how strong to dece weomen are, against whose engins, a m will, is noe sure defence

3 *Objection answered* [marginal note].

[adds "not," to read]
3 *Objection* not *answered.*

For the third objection, *It is good for a man not touch a woman:* The Apostle makes it not a positive prohibition, but speakes it onelie because of the *Corinths* present necessitie, who were then persecuted by the enemies of the Church, for which cause, and no other, hee saith, *Art thou loosed from a wife: seeke not a wife:* meaning whilst the time of these per-turbations should continue in their heate; *but if thou art bound, seeke not to be loosed: if thou marriest, thou sinnest not,* only increasest thy

[adds "to," to read] not to touch
that is, sinfully or incontinently

This piece of scripture, like a two ed sworde, hath cutt you into the Graine, wh makes you give this false exposition: for Apostle speaketh this, to admonish us to chastly for what meomets bee when he sa I would that all men weare even as I my s am: That is, not only single man, but

for the married careth for the things of
world, And I wish that you were without
that yee might cleave fast unto the Lord
out separation: For the time remaineth,
they which have wives be as though they
none: for the persecuters shall deprive
of them, eyther by imprisonment, ban-
ment, or death; so that manifest it is, that
Apostle doth not heereby forbid mar-
e, but onely adviseth the *Corinths* to for-
e a while, till God in mercie should
e the fury of their adversaries.

fourth and last objection, is that of
mon, *I have found one man among a thou-*
l, but a woman among them all have I not
d: for answere of which, if we looke into
storie of his life, wee shall finde therein a
mmentary upon this enigmaticall Sen-
e included: for it is there said, that
mon had seven hundred wives, and three
dred concubines, which number con-
d make one thousand. These women
ing his heart away from being perfect
the Lord his God, sufficient cause had
to say, that among the said thousand
nen found he not one upright. Hee saith
that among a thousand women never any
found one worthy of commendation,
speakes in the first person singularly, *I*
not found, meaning in his owne experi-
e: for this assertion is to be holden a part
ne confession of his former follies, and no
rwise, his repentance being the intended
of *Ecclesiastes.*

ill proceede toward the period of my
nded taske, which is, to decipher the
llency of women:

efficient cause of womans creation, was
vah the *Eternall*...That worke then can
chuse but be good, yea very good, which
rought by so excellent a workeman as the
d: for he being a glorious Creator, must
les effect a worthie creature.

chast[e], which was a proper guift of God
given unto him:

If the wisest man that ever lived, in [choos-
inge] of seven hundred wives & three hundred concubines, could not choose one that
was upright: what s[h]ould wee silly men
hope for a good woeman in these our latter
dayes. 37

Proprio Laus, Sordet in ore. 38

That worke can not choose butt bee badd, yea 39
verie b[add] which woeman hath wrought
her selfe: for since he framd her, she hath
p[ut] new colours of white and red upon hir
face; sett in new teethe, either weares not hir
own naturall haire, or if it bee, itt is soe
powd[red] and soe perfumed, that as, shee
thinkes, shee hath much mended hir crea-
tours werke. Had theie [con]tinued as theie
weare at the first created, they had binn excellent: butt the manie are soe chaunged in face,
that you shall scarse knowe them from a Pa[?]

Secondly, the materiall cause, or matter whereof woman was made, was of a refined mould, if I may so speake: for man was created of the dust of the earth, but woman was made of a part of man…This being rightly considered, doth teach men to make such account of their wives, as *Adam* did of *Eve, This is bone of my bone, and flesh of my flesh:* As also, that they neyther doe or wish any more hurt unto them, then unto their owne bodies: for men ought to love their wives as themselves, because hee <u>that loves his wife, loves himselfe:</u> And never man hated his owne flesh (which the woman is) unlesse a monster in nature.

Likewise hee that loves himselfe; love wife; and therefore, how comes it to p that manie men care not for their wifes notwithstanding love themselves in the ▶ est degree. allsoe that woemen complaine want of love in theire [hu]sbandes tow: them.

Thirdly, the formall cause, fashion, and proportion of woman was excellent:…For as God gave man a lofty countenance, that hee might looke up toward Heaven, so did he likewise give unto woman. And as the temperature of mans body is excellent, so is womans. For whereas other Creatures, <u>by reason of their grosse humours,</u> have excrements for their habite, as foules, their feathers, beasts, their haire, fishes, their scales, man and woman onely, have their skinne cleare and smoothe. And (that more is) in the Image of God were they both created; yea and to be briefe, <u>all the parts of their bodies,</u> both externall and internall, were correspondent and meete each for other.

they wanted Reason, which should t them to provide for themselves; and there god and Nature provided for them.

[comment crossed out]

Fourthly and lastly, the finall cause, or end, for which woman was made, was to glorifie God, and to be a collaterall companion for man to glorifie God, in using her bodie, and all the parts, powers, and faculties thereof, as instruments for his honour: As with her voice to sound foorth his prayses, like *Miriam,* and the rest of her company;

Sutch theie should bee, & not sutch as ¢ are.

with her tongue not to utter words of strife, but to give good councell unto her husband, the which hee must not despise.

Finally, no power externall or internall <u>ought</u> woman to keep idle, but to imploy it in some service of GOD, to the glorie of her Creator, and comfort of her owne soule.

You commende those where never anie commende. butt sett mee forthe sutch a ¥ man as one of these now livinge.

It was the sayenge of Seneca, Longum est per praecepta; breve et efficex per exem Shewe them, by your example, and lett y deedes speake unto them: Plus sonas (v metuo) quam vales.

The <u>other end</u> for which woman was made, was to be a Companion and *helper* for man;

A woeman was made for both endes.

erefore *Salomon* saith, <u>*Woe to him that is*</u>
<u>*e;*</u> for when thoughts of discomfort, trou-
of this world, and feare of dangers do
sesse him, he wants a companion to lift
up from the pit of perplexitie, into which
is fallen:

Oh, for a husbande.   47

a good wife, saith *Plautus,* is the wealth of
minde, and the welfare of the heart; and
refore a meete <u>associate for her husband;</u>
l *Woman,* saith *Paul, is the glorie of the man.*

You pleade well for a husbande; & it is a great   48
pittie, that you have not had a good one long
since.

rriage is a <u>merri-age,</u> and this worlds Para-
e, where there is mutuall love. Our blessed
iour vouchsafed to honour a marriage
h the first miracle that he wrought, unto
ich miracle matrimoniall estate may not
itly bee resembled:

See how shee is carried away in a golden dis-   49
traction: you must goe to Man, or all will bee
spoyled.

as Christ turned water into wine, a farre
re excellent liquor; which, as the Psalmist
h, <u>*Makes glad the heart of man;*</u>

Oh, for a husbande.   50

the single man is by marriage changed
m a <u>Batchelour to a Husband,</u> a farre more
ellent title:

This is just as our old proverbe is; out of the   51
fryinge pan into the fire.

m a solitarie life unto a joyfull union and
junction, with such a creature as God
h made <u>meete for man,</u> for whom none
s meete till shee was made.

Maydenhead for a husband.   52

vertuous woman, saith *Salomon, is the*
wne of her husband; By which metaphor
sheweth both the excellencie of such a
e, and what account her husband is to
ke of her:

Shee is the crowne of her husbande: for as   53
manie, & as great cares doe attende uppon a
married man, as do uppon the crowne of a
kinge.

r a King doth not trample his <u>Crowne</u>
der his feete, but highly esteemes of it, gen-
handles it, and carefully laies it up, as the
dence of his Kingdome;

The man is the head, and you would faine bee   54
the crown[e] on the topp of his heade; you
suckt that ambition from your first parent.

<u>husbands should not</u> account their wives
their vassals, but as those that are heires
ether of the grace of life,

You make your way, against you gett a hus-   55
bande.

l with all lenitie and milde perswasions set
ir feete in the right way, if they happen to
ad awry, bearing with their infirmities, as
anah did with his wives barrennesse.

Theye tread theire shar[e?] awry oftentimes.   56

e Kingdome of God is compared unto the
rriage of a Kings sonne:

This booke will bespea[ke] you a husband.   57

Thus if men would remember the <u>duties</u> they are to performe in being heads, some would not stand a tip-toe as they doe, thinking themselves Lords and Rulers,

Surely now I must thinke that either yo⌐ married, or fayrely promised for now comend the[se]. and I wishe that your bande, will learne this good lesson.

But least I should seeme too partiall in praysing women so much as I have (though no more then warrant from Scripture doth allow) I adde to the premises, that <u>I say not, all women are vertuous,</u> for then they should be more excellent then men, sith of *Adams* sonnes there was *Cain* as well as *Abel,*

For sayenge soe your tongue should Lye s⌐

so that of men as of women, there are two sorts, namely, <u>good and bad,</u>

of a bad man and a bad woeman, which i⌐ best.

And if women were not sinfull, then should they not <u>need a Saviour:</u> but the Virgin *Mary* a patterne of piety, *rejoyced in God her Saviour: Ergo,* she was a sinner.

This argument is needelesse, for whoe yett denyed but weomen weare sinfull.

In the *Revelation* the Church is called the Spouse of Christ; and in *Zachariah,* <u>wickednesse is called a woman,</u> to shew that of women there are both godly and ungodly:

Qoate mee a place of scripture wheare m⌐ called by sutch a name

But farre be it from any one, to condemne the righteous with the wicked, <u>or good</u> women with the bad (as the Bayter of women doth:)

There is noe one that either is, or doth g⌐ noe, not one

Of the good sort is it that I have in this booke spoken, and so would I that all that reade it should so understand me: for if otherwise I had done, I should have incurred that woe, which by the Prophet *Isaiah* is pronounced against them that *speake well of evill,* and should have *justified the wicked, which thing is abhominable to the Lord.*

In which of these sorts doe you include y⌐ selfe: if amongst the good; then do you ju⌐ fie your selfe. if amongst those which are e⌐ then need wee noe farther wittnes. The⌐ noe Medium.

THE EPILOGUE

Great was the unthankefulnesse of *Pharaohs* Butler unto *Joseph*...But farre greater is the ingratitude of those men toward God, that dare presume to speake and exclaime against *Woman,* whom God did create for mans comfort. What greater discredit can redound to a workeman, then to have the man, for whom hee hath made it, say, it is naught?

A Man may with scripture reproove weom⌐ for in Manie places therin they are sett f⌐ in theire colours.

CERTAINE QUAERES
TO THE READER

Although (curteous Reader) <u>I am young in yeares</u>, and more defective in knowledge, that

Virgo pudicitiam notat aetatemq[ue] pud⌐ You speak like a mayd, not like a Virgin. I⌐

smattering in Learning which I have
ined, being only the fruit of such vacant
res, as I could spare from affaires befitting
Sex,

AERES

bee true, asse you affirme, Page 2. line 26.
t *women will not give thankes for a good*
e.
demand whether *Deborah* and *Hannah*
not women, who both of them sang
nes of thankesgiving unto the Lord;

where-asse you say, Page 4. line 22. *that a*
an that hath a faire face, it is ever matched
a cruel heart, and her heavenly lookes with
sh thoughts: You therein shew your selfe a
radictor of Scriptures presidents: For
ail was a beautifull woman, and tender-
ted; *Rebekah* was both faire of face and
full.

or your audacitie in judging of womens
ghts, you thereby shew your selfe an
per against the King of heaven, the true
wledge of cogitations being appropriate
him alone.

ur assertion, That *a woman is better lost*
found, better forsaken then taken (Page 5.
4.) be to be credited, me thinkes, great
y it is, that afore you were borne, there was
e so wise as to counsell your father not to
dle with a woman, that hee might have
ped those troubles, which you affirme,
all married men are cumbred with, Page
ne 20.

lso that hee might not have begotten such
onster in nature *Asse* your selfe,

the Priest which forgot he was Parish
arke) defame and exclaime against
nen, as though your selfe had never had a
her, or you never beene a child.

aying (Page 10. line. 25.) that *Jobs wife*
selled her husband to curse God, you misconster the Text; for the true construction

---

young sir and scorne affection; 'um, 'um,
'um.

Two amongst tenne thousande: the authors 67
meaning is, of those weomen [that] now live
in these our days. Likewise when he speaketh
of weomen hee doth not meane all weomen
for that weare too absurde; butt [woe]men for
the most part, are soe.

Still you bringe in examples of the dayes of 68
olde. butt it is not sayde that theye then weare
soe; butt that most part of those which now
live, are soe.

[comment crossed out, illegible] 69

Her thoughts manie times looke out att her 70
Eyes, & come fourth in her wordes. Besides
you may if you please, enter into her minde by
hir bodyes gate; and have them all, sutch as
they are.

There is a singular worde pointinge at a singu- 71
lar ill-conditioned woeman.

Asses have four leggs and hee hath but two: 72
Crisse-crosse Kisse his Asse and make not
sutch a Doe.

You have forgott that you are a priest daugh- 73
ter, for instead of preachinge you rayle right
downe.

If you conster this aright, then have I binne 74
taught amisse: butt I had rather beeleeve a
sound devine, then a shallow woeman.

thereof will shew it to bee a <u>*Sarcasmus* or *Ironicall* speech,</u> and not an instigation to blasphemie.

Page 11. line 8. you count it *Wonderfull to see the mad feates of women, for shee will now bee merry, then sad:* but me thinkes it is farre more *wonder-foole* to have one, that adventures to make his Writing as publique as an In-keepers Signe, which hangs to the view of all passengers, to want Grammaticall Concordance in his said Writing, and joyne together *Women* plurall, and *shee* singular, *Asse* you not onely in this place, but also in others have done.

Now the foole rides you, for that was printers fault in puttinge in Woman for men.

have you not feared blasphemously to say, *that women sprung from the divell,* Page 15. line 26. But being, as it seemes, defective in that whereof you have much need (for *mendacem oportet esse memorem*) you suddainely after say, That *women were created by God, and formed by nature, and therefore by policie and wisedome to be avoyded,* Page 16. line 12. An impious conclusion to inferre, that because God created, therefore to be avoyded: Oh intollerable absurdity!

To be avoyded, is as much as to say avoyd [that] is, that men are able to avoyd ther polycy and wisdome. And therefore frame that Indication, of your owne mi derstandinge. O weake and ignorant wo

<u>*Men I say may live without women,*</u> *but women cannot live without men,* Page 14. line 18. If any Religious Author had thus affirmed, I should have wondred, that unto Satans suggestions he had so much subjected himselfe, as to crosse the Almighties providence and care for mans good, who positively said, <u>*It is not good for man to bee alone;*</u>

That you may see dayly, that men may without weomen: Wheather that sayenge only concerne Adam, whoe then was alo will not argue: Butt surely I thinke It wa ment of all men: for manie have both and dyed single men; and without questi was good for them, soe to bee alone.

But being that the sole testimony heereof is your owne *dico,* I marvell no whit at the errour, but heartily wish, that unto all the untruths you have uttered in your infamous booke, you had subscribed your <u>*Dico,*</u> that none of them might bee adjudged truths: For <u>*mendacis praemium est verbis eius non adhiberi fidem.*</u>

Let his Dixit stand for his Dico. for he spoken them. yett for charities sake bee him, if hee sayes hee loves you not.

Therefore stay not alone in the company of a woman, trusting to thy owne chastity, except thou bee more strong then Sampson, *more wise then* Salomon, *or more holy then* David, *for these, and many more have beene overcome by the sweete intisements of women,* Page 22.

I may as well say *Barrabas* was a murtherer, *Joab* killed *Abner* and *Amasa*...; therefore stay

alone in the companie of a man, trusting
hy owne strength, except thou bee stron-
then *Josiah*, and more valiant then *Abner
Amasa*, for these and many more have
ne murthered by men. The forme of argu-
itation is your owne, the which if you dis-
, blame your selfe for proposing such a
erne, and blush at your owne folly.

e 31. line 15. *If God had not made women
ly to bee a plague to man, hee would never
e called them necessarie evils.* Albeit I have
read *Seaton* or *Ramus,* nor so much as
ie (though heard of) *Aristotles Organon,*
by that I have seene and reade in compasse
ny apprehension, I will adventure to frame
irgument or two, to shew what danger, for
your blasphemy you are in.
o fasten a lie upon God is blasphemy: But
Bayter of women fastens a lie upon God:
, the *Bayter* is a blasphemer.

ou marryest a still and a quiet woman, that
seeme to thee that thou ridest but an
bling horse to hell, but if with one that is fro-
rd and unquiet, then thou wert as good ride a
ting horse to the divell.* Page 35. line 13.
this your affirmation be true, then seemes
hat hell is the period of all married mens
vailes, and the center of their circumfer-
e. A man can but have either a good wife or
ad; and if he have the former, you say he
h but seeme to amble to hell; if the latter,
were as good trot to the divell: But if mar-
l men ride, how travaile Batchelours?
ely, by your rule they must go on foote,
ause they want wives; which (inclusively)
i say are like horses to carry their husbands
hell. Wherefore in my minde, it was not
hout mature consideration that you mar-
l in time, because it would be too irkesome
you to travaile so tedious a journey on
te.

e will make thee weare an Oxe feather in thy
ope.* Page 44. line 4.
Oxen have feathers, their haires more fitly
y be so termed then their hornes.

e 51. *line* 16. *Many are the joyes and sweete
asures in Marriage, as in our children, etc.*

You have wisely prooved that you have played   79
the foole for companie: and I see that you will
rather[.] and indeede I thinke you are better
able to follow a foole, then to leade him.

It is not good for man to bee alone Gene: 2:   80
28. Therefor[e] theie are necessarie. That
the[ie] are evill, I neede bringe no proofe.
Therefore to fasten a lye uppon a man is a sure
token of a wicked [dis]position.

Hell is not the period of married mens   81
travayles, but a place the which, in his way
to Heaven, hee must of necessitie, passe
thourough. For that is the neerest and reddiest
way to Heaven: Butt wheather theire wives
amble or trott with them, theie themselves
know best. Then you aske the quaestion how
Batchelours travayle; why surely theie ride
too, for companies sake, uppon sutch coltes as
you are. Whoe neither amble nor trott per-
fectly, butt ride a good fayr gallop to the devill,
and there wee have you.

If married men ride, how travayle Batche-   82
lours: Why surely say you theie must goe on
foot bycause theie want wives: butt I have
prooved the contrarie, and have found them
naggs to ride. Then thus I say: if married men
bee theire wives Heads, then what head have
Maides. why surely none, bycause they want
Husbands.

You interprett the Hornes to be feathers, &   83
not the author himselfe. This is the virtue of a
guiltie conscience. Heu quam difficile est cri-
men non prodere verbis.

[A line in the margin beside these several con-   84
tradictory quotes from Swetnam presumably

Page 34. line 5. There are many troubles comes gallopping at the heeles of a woman. If thou wert a Servant, or in bondage afore, yet when thou marriest, thy toyle is never the nearer ended, but even then, and not before, thou changest thy golden life, which thou didst leade before (in respect of the married) for a droppe of hony, which quickely turnes to be as bitter as worme-wood.

Page 53. line 19. The husband ought (in signe of love) to impart his secrets and counsell unto his wife, for many have found much comfort and profite by taking their wives counsell; and if thou impart any ill happe to thy wife, shee lighteneth thy griefe, either by comforting thee lovingly, or else, in bearing a part thereof patiently.

Page 41. line 12. If thou unfouldest any thing of secret to a woman, the more thou chargest her to keepe it close, the more shee will seeme, as it were, with childe, till shee have revealed it.

It was the saying of a judicious Writer, that whoso makes the fruit of his cogitations extant to the view of all men, should have his worke to be as a well tuned Instrument, in all places according and agreeing, the which I am sure yours doth not: For how <u>reconcile</u> you those dissonant places above cited?

wishing unto every such *Misogunes*, a *Tiburne Tiffenie* for curation of his swolne necke, which onely through a Cynicall inclination will not indure the yoke of lawfull Matrimony, I bid farewell.

indicates that his comment below pertai[n] them all]

Ironia Dicta

Theie are butt soe manie pills overspr[ead] with hony which you havinge soe gree[dily] gaped after; and now swallowed, have g[iven] you this gentle vomitt, & made your ton[gue] voyde of evill wordes. [the rest crossed out illegible]

How can shee in the first place wishe a h[alter] on him, and then afterward bid him farew[ell] Unlesse shee speake that inhumane prove[rb] Farewell & bee hang'd.

Notes to the Marginalia

nber 19. **Philogunes:** lover of women (Greek).

nber 24. **Carri-age:** She is old enough to carry herself well (sexually).

nber 27. **prizz:** prize (in a sexual combat).

nber 36. **meomets:** moments.

nber 38. **Propio...ore:** Praise for one's own is foul in the mouth.

nber 45. **Longum...exempla:** The way is long through precept; short and efficacious ugh example. **Plus...vales:** You speak more (I greatly fear) than you are able to do.

nber 66. **Virgo...puella:** A virgin is characterized by chastity, a young girl simply by age.

nber 78. **Let his Dixit stand for his Dico:** Let his "it is said" stand for "I say," i.e., let all his ments be as if he had explicitly proclaimed them his own with "I say."

nber 83. **Heu quam difficile...verbis:** Oh how difficult it is not to publish our guilt by our ds.

nber 85. **Ironia Dicta:** an ironic speech.

Printed in the United States
858400002B

9 780195 086157